Maine to
CAPE HORN

Maine to CAPE HORN

The World's Most Dangerous Voyage

CHARLES H. LAGERBOM

THE History PRESS

Published by The History Press
Charleston, SC
www.historypress.com

First published 2021

Manufactured in the United States

ISBN 9781467150057

Library of Congress Control Number: 2021938385

Notice: The information in this book is true and complete to the best of our knowledge. It is offered without guarantee on the part of the author or The History Press. The author and The History Press disclaim all liability in connection with the use of this book.

My father helped me appreciate the lessons of history, the lure of adventure and the call of the sea. I am proud to share his name as well as his love of a good story. This is for him.

CONTENTS

ACKNOWLEDGEMENTS

Thank you to the following for your assistance and support in researching, writing and preparing this work, including those who are no longer with us (*).

Spencer Apollonio; Gary Bennett; Eric Berryman*; John F. Berube; Keith Brann; Bob Dale*; Jon Cox; Paul C. Dalrymple*; John Dearborn*; Susan Devlin; John Golden, PMM; Cipperly Good, PMM; Chris Grallert; Steve Hutchings; Ross and Zoe James; Kevin Johnson, PMM; Marvin Kenney; Audrey C. Lagerbom; C.E. Lagerbom; Jay Morrison; Ken Moulton*; Kelly Page, MMM; Megan Pinette, Belfast Historical Society and Museum; Christophe Pollet; Bob Rutford*; Stephen Sanfilippo; Bill Spindler; John Splettstoesser*; Sarah Timm, MMM; Ed Varney; Matt Winters; and Dick Wolak.

A special thank-you to my wife, Jennifer, and children, Audrey and Charlie.

INTRODUCTION

Cape Horn: that not-so-lofty mountain is represented in every sailor's soul.
—Thomas Wells

Cape Horn's and Maine's maritime histories are linked, fused by wooden ships, seasoned sea captains, intrepid mariners and hardy sailors of the Pine Tree State. My own visits there have been mercifully brief with decent weather, but with those gray seas, one can feel the presence of countless vessels and mariners who sailed these waters in far more challenging conditions. Some visitors suggest it is the light, wind or weird landscape that affects them. There definitely is a poignancy to the Horn; loneliness hangs heavy as the weather, melancholy with its remoteness, churning waters, cry of sea birds and constant winds. Truly *fin del mundo*, or world's end, that faraway place, both geographically and emotionally, that can test one's mettle and sear the soul. One stands in awe of mariners who did it the old way—the hard way.

Cape Horn has earned a prominent place in art, song, literature and Maine seafaring history. Long recognized as a maritime touchstone for sailors, Cape Stiff still haunts the imagination. Doubling Cape Horn became the ultimate test of faith, hardihood and seamanship. A true test for a mariner, it earned them an exclusive badge of honor, a most-prized singular achievement. Those who were successful entered a privileged club. In the 1840s, Cape Horn veterans from Maine could be recognized

by a gold earring in their left ear. Having doubled the Horn, they were allowed to put their feet on the table while dining—both if they also rounded the Cape of Good Hope. The earring testified to their success at surviving that stretch of water, the most dangerous on the planet. Captain Harvey Mills of St. George displays his earring in an 1847 painting at the Maine Maritime Museum. Mills went to sea at twelve and was captain by twenty-five. In 1872, before retiring, he brought the ship *Eliza McNeil* from New York to San Francisco in 119 days, which was respectable for a non-clipper. Other Mainers, not as successful, never returned from such troubled waters. This is why their earring was gold; it covered the cost of a funeral should the mariner's body ever be recovered.[1]

A portrait of mariner Harvey Mills, circa 1847, with his Cape Horn gold earring. *Courtesy of the Maine Maritime Museum.*

Other Mainers share this connection with Cape Horn. Thomaston's Captain James Watts was only nineteen when he took the *John T. Henry* around the Horn. Searsport's Lincoln R. Colcord, the son of Maine mariner Lincoln A. Colcord, entered the world in Cape Horn waters. On August 14, 1883, he was born aboard *Charlotte A. Littlefield* while his father battled through a storm. Lincoln R. Colcord died on November 16, 1947, at the age of sixty-four and was buried in Searsport's Elmwood Cemetery, same location as Captain Jesse Thayer Carver, a Maine native who risked everything on a Cape Horn voyage. Aside from his maritime pedigree, Lincoln R. Colcord is known for writing "Maine Stein Song" for the university, which was popularized by another Mainer, Rudy Vallée.[2]

In the 1930s, Colcord corresponded with a Lorena Protheroe, the daughter of a maritime family who was familiar with Cape Horn and square-rigged ships. At the time, she was working on a book on the "blue-water women" who helped their husbands on difficult voyages. In a letter to Colcord, she noted with displeasure a potential publisher's lack of interest and their suggestion about Cape Horn voyages tending to be repetitious or lacking drama.

> *I don't understand that, except that there were different angles of Cape Horn voyages—I thought them quite different...wow! And they had*

> *included accounts of Mrs. Patten's taking command of the Neptune's Car, of Miss Armstrong's command when almost all hands had come down with yellow fever and her mother had died, of Mrs. Oakes' terrible experience alone in the cabin when her husband's ship was lost off the horn...repetitious? To my mind, scarcely. Horn passages, yes, from such very different angles to the same view. I guess it would take a Cape Horner to appreciate them, though.*[3]

Mainers and Maine-built ships labored in those waters, and some never came back. Horn casualties, whether ship or man, resulted in many empty graves back in Maine, only a headstone and a "lost at sea" inscription to tell the tale.

What is it about Cape Horn that makes men willingly put themselves through such an ordeal? What emerges is an exciting story of bold Mainers and dangerous voyages. It's all just part of the job, yet it's an exhilarating and deadly dance with danger. Cape Horn might offer redemption, salvation, financial security and success, but it also came with failure, destruction, injury, financial ruin and death. Certainly, it was high-risk and high-reward, but was it repetitious or lacking in drama? Let the reader be the judge.

1
THE END OF THE EARTH

Off Cape Horn, there are but two kinds of weather,
neither one of them a pleasant kind.
—John Masefield

By the late eighteenth century, greater numbers of American sailing ships faced Cape Horn to enter Pacific waters. Whalers interested in reaching the South Pacific, traders on the China Run, guano trade carriers and ships involved in American seal trade off of the California Coast all took the Cape Horn route. They went in many Maine-built ships, with captains hailing from Maine and crews including many native Mainers. These connections between the state and a windswept dangerous cape at South America's southern extremity helped shape Maine maritime history.

In 1914, however, the Panama Canal opened for business. This engineering marvel, a carved pathway across the continent, allowed for faster access between Atlantic and Pacific Oceans. It also shaved eight thousand miles off of an ocean voyage from New York City to San Francisco—a game changer technologically, economically and culturally. Before the Panama Canal and transcontinental railroads connected America's eastern and western shores, there were only three ways to get to the Pacific Coast. Overland by foot or wagon was dangerous and time-consuming. Another way was to sail to Panama, cross the jungle isthmus and then hope to find a vessel heading north on the Pacific side. The best option was to double Cape Horn.

The Chilean station on Hoorn Island. *From the collection of John Splettstoesser, courtesy of the Antarctican Society.*

In 1522, explorer Ferdinand Magellan sailed to find the southern end of the American landmass. Fighting weather, mutinous crews and unknown waters, he discovered straits that now bear his name. After a stormy month-long transit, he emerged into the Pacific Ocean, which he named after spending weeks in the turbulent strait. His achievement was magnificent, but it did not answer whether the continent ended or continued southward.[4]

In 1578, Francis Drake took eighteen days to struggle through the Strait of Magellan. He was not prepared for the fifty-two days of storms he encountered upon leaving the inland passage's relative safety. This was no "Pacific" ocean. Fierce weather drove them far southward, and Drake enshrined his name on the turbulent stretch of water separating South America from the Antarctic Peninsula, the infamous Drake Passage. It also spawned debate over whether Drake was the first to discover Cape Horn or if he landed on the actual island itself?[5]

The recorded discovery and first westbound passage of Cape Horn went to Willem Schouten of the Netherlands. Schouten named the headland island Hoorn after his hometown in Holland as well as one of his ships. He

had to madly tack back and forth in front of the Horn amid cold weather, variable winds, huge waves, hail and rain. After he was finally able to round the Horn on January 31, 1616, Schouten's chart, due to lousy weather, showed an incomplete chunk of land. He was not sure if it was an island or something larger. Schouten did prove a ship could work its way westward and successfully double this extreme southern point.[6]

Cape Horn could be navigated, but it was not easy, and it was further complicated by constant bad weather, difficult seas and challenging winds. While James Cook successfully followed in Schouten's tracks, the Horn defied William Bligh of HMS *Bounty* in March 1788. Adverse winds forced him back into the Atlantic Ocean, so he opted for the Cape of Good Hope route instead.[7]

The actual island of Cape Horn is a member of the Hermite Cluster, many with steep evergreen-shrouded mountainsides. Whether or not Drake landed there, its only reasonable anchorage is Caleta Leon, but it offers little protection and is a poor holding ground. Above the tide line, a wooden stairway leads up a steep mossy hill to a boardwalk that was built to prevent trampling the tussock grass. It leads to a small Chilean station that is mostly for tourists, but it also marks possession from Argentina. The place is weather-beaten; a small post office provides official Cape Horn stamps and postcards. Nearby is a small chapel. The actual cape is about one and a half miles due southwest across the island, beyond a little bay. From the stairs and the boardwalk, Cape Horn's seaward side is not visible, only its backside, which is fitting, since experiencing Cape Horn from the seaward side is what it was all about.[8]

In 1992, a large memorial was added; a seven-meter-tall sculpture by Chilean artist José Balcells, made of ten steel plates, each six millimeters thick, that shows a flying albatross. The dedication reads, "To the memory of the men of the sea from every nation that lost their lives fighting against the merciless forces of nature of the Southern Ocean that prevail in the vicinity of the legendary Cape Horn." While it was built to withstand 125-mile-per-hour wind gusts, in 2014, terrific winds knocked it over.[9] On another marble slab is a poem by Chilean writer Sara Vial.

> *I am the albatross that awaits you at the end of the earth. I am the forgotten soul of the dead sailors who sailed around Cape Horn from all the seas of the world. But they did not die in the furious waves, today they fly on my wings, toward eternity, in the last crevasse of the Antarctic winds.*[10]

Antarctic field guide John Splettstoesser at Cape Horn Station. *From the collection of John Splettstoesser, courtesy of the Antarctican Society.*

A postcard of the Cape Horn memorial. *From the collection of Charles H. Lagerbom.*

Cape Horn is known for birds, many which accompanied the sailing ships. One sailor said there were so many feathers on the water that the surface looked like foam. The most prominent of these birds is the albatross, hence the choice for monument. The snowy wandering albatross (*Diomedea exulans*) is the largest, whitest wanderer and has the longest wingspan, which can reach twelve feet. Considered the most efficient traveler of the world's vertebrates, they can hover for hours on the windward side, between the masts of a sailing ship, remaining almost motionless. They use techniques known as dynamic soaring and slope soaring, expending zero energy for an almost unlimited amount of time. Sailors caught them with fishhooks baited with pieces of salt pork, although Coleridge's warning springs to mind. Their wing bones were used as pipe filters or for masts and spars on model ships. A dried foot on a string could also be used to store a few ounces of fat.[11]

The albatross, symbol of a dead seaman's soul, adorns the members' badge of the Amicale Internationale des Capitaines au Long Course—Cap Horniers. Known as the Cape Horners organization, it was started in 1936 in St. Malo, Brittany, as an attempt to recognize captains and crews of square-rigged ships that rounded Cape Horn. One international grand master said Cape Horn is as symbol of a vanished era, a reminder of an age when men worked together fighting the most primitive forces of nature and a mark of nostalgia toward youth, "whereby young sailing captains and their crews were able to exert their enthusiasm to penetrate the utmost secrets of the winds and seas throughout the world in order to carry the great white ships to every corner." In 1983, they gathered on the Italian Riviera for the Thirty-Fourth Annual Congress of Cape Horners. There were 320 members present, with an average age of eighty. One participant lamented their dwindling number by referring to the famous line: "And then there were none."[12]

Cape Horn is located at 56 degrees south latitude, the very end of South America's continental landmass. Interestingly, it shares the 67 degrees west longitude line with Cutler, Maine. A direct north–south distance of just under seven thousand miles separates the two locations. The Horn brings to mind visions of wind-whipped water, plunging seas, desperate mariners hanging aloft in frozen rigging, braving howling winds and flapping sails. It marks where Pacific and Atlantic waters meet in one writhing mass. Why is the passage so stormy and dangerous? The area receives precipitation 278 days a year, producing annual rainfall totals of eighty inches or almost seven feet of water. Average temperatures hover around 40 degrees Fahrenheit.[13]

South of Cape Horn, Drake Passage stretches from 60 degrees south to 70 degrees south latitude. This expanse of water continues completely free of land around the entire planet, encircling Antarctica to the south. Such an open passage allows for a truly free maritime highway, as the wind and waves and storms constantly remain active and in motion. The Drake Passage acts as a funnel for these winds, waves and water. The meeting of the Pacific and Atlantic Oceans off the Horn also produces an extreme low-pressure weather system, hallmark of treacherous seas. Storms are called graybeards or Cape Horn snorters, and winds are known as williwaws or woollies. There are plenty of both. Then there are the furious fifties and screaming sixties. Prevailing winds howl out of the west on uninterrupted circles of the planet, constantly pushing vessels back eastward, hence the square-riggers' obsession to make westing.[14]

Westbound sailing ships have to constantly tack to make way into such headwinds. The result is a frustrating back-and-forth dance to gain minimal distance while hoping decent weather holds. Sailing directions for Cape Horn remain pretty simple: make westing—whatever you do, make westing. It's not as easy as it sounds, as prevailing winds shriek out of the west, right into one's teeth. The phrase "doubling Cape Horn" refers to the time it took a vessel to cross 50 degrees south latitude on one side of South America heading south, until it crossed that line again on the other side heading north. Rates of progress were recorded and compared; then bragging or lamenting began. At a distance of 930 miles, success was measured in the fewest days it took to cross that 50 degree line again.[15]

Competition could be fierce. In 1851, three clipper ships heading toward Cape Horn, converging on a southerly heading, found themselves in a race. There was *Raven* and *Seawitch* and the Kittery-built clipper *Typhoon*. The 1,610-ton *Typhoon* was 225 feet long and had been built by the Fernald & Pettigrew Shipyard. Classed as an extreme clipper, *Typhoon* was fully rigged while on the stocks, and it was launched with skysail-yards aloft and colors flying. It had a thirty-inch dead-rise, which produced little roll or wallow. Such a V shape allowed quick movement through water. On its maiden Horn voyage, *Typhoon* posted a ten-day doubling of Cape Horn.[16]

But in 1851, all three vessels weathered Cape St. Roque and stood away southward for the three-thousand-mile dash through the southeast trades. They all crossed 50 degrees south in same longitude line, 64 degrees west. *Raven* gained a day on *Sea Witch*, and the two were in sight of each other, side by side. *Typhoon* sailed 2 days astern. The crews prepared for the Horn, putting extra lashings on anything that might break loose from

rough seas. Westerly gales lashed them for two weeks. *Sea Witch* and *Raven* fought for distance, each tack trying to gain the advantage. Both lofted most of their sails, almost too much for such conditions. *Typhoon*, under Charles H. Salter of Portsmouth, slowly closed the distance. Finally, *Sea Witch* and *Raven* doubled the Horn, both having taken two weeks. *Typhoon* gained another day and was within twenty-four hours of them. *Typhoon* reached San Francisco in 108 days, one day behind the others. In another race in 1853, against clipper *Simoon*, *Typhoon* came in again one day later, compelled to stand off in fog before entering port. In 1863, *Typhoon* was sold in Singapore. By 1869, it was British owned renamed *Indomitable.*[17]

Progress in 1914 of the Maine-built down-easter *Edward Sewall* was completely different. Under Captain Richard Quick, it endlessly tacked, trying to get westward, but it had little success. It crossed 50 degrees south on March 7 and recrossed the line May 12. Quick had had to take fifty-four different courses covering twenty thousand running miles, and the entire voyage lasted 293 days. It took the ship 67 days to double Cape Horn, logging five thousand miles, three times normal distance.[18] Fast passages

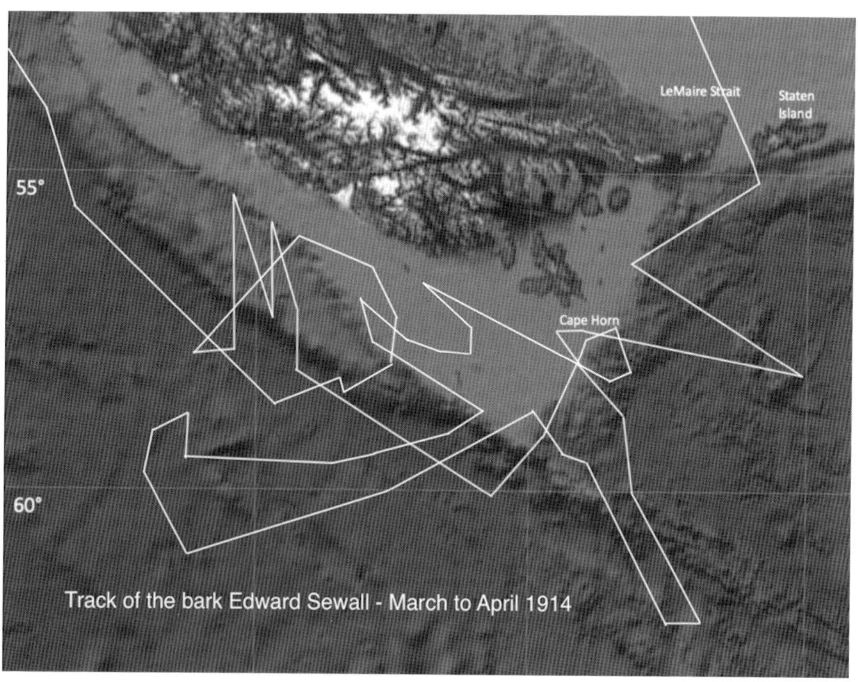

Track of the Maine-built bark *Edward Sewall* showing the difficulty of trying to make westing to get around Cape Horn. *Produced by the author.*

were noted for their rarity, seamanship or luck. Longer passages were due to many factors.

One danger was shipping heavy seas. Rogue waves off Cape Horn can measure ninety-eight feet. If the entire port or starboard side is submerged, seas can literally drag a ship over and under. Shipping waves made footing along the deck extremely dangerous. Safety netting was established along bulwarks, and lines were affixed to haul oneself along. Stewards used them to deliver meals to captain and crew, but still, many meals (and sailors) were washed overboard. In February 1890, 1,788-ton Maine-built *Carleton* took one month to battle the Horn. In 1895, it was pooped by a monstrous wave, which meant a wave took it from astern, sweeping its entire length. Such a wave could easily destroy a ship's steering gear. *Carleton*'s wheelhouse and wheel were totally smashed, and its compass was washed away. The mate was killed, one helmsman broke his arm and another was knocked unconscious. *Carleton*'s captain, North Haven's Edwin T. Amesbury, improvised a wheel, fashioned a steering compass and successfully completed the voyage.[19]

Helmsmen often required another set of hands to help steer while in Cape Horn waters. A ship's wheel could spin uncontrollably, handles or grips could easily snap an arm or wrist. On one occasion, two helmsmen, with straps over their shoulders that were secured to pad-eyes on the deck, grimly held on to the wheel. But they could not even communicate; one later recalled that every time he opened his mouth to speak, howling winds blew his cheeks out. Other accounts tell of a helmsman being flipped over a free-spinning wheel or flung across deck. Poor visibility and turbulent conditions also made taking navigation sights extremely difficult. Glimpses of sun, horizon or stars—necessary to maintain position and chart one's passage—were rare. Routes were often remeasured and more accurately replotted long after their time in Cape Horn waters.[20]

From the roaring forties southward, the weather can change quickly, and it often does. Antarctic ocean currents flow opposite to the predominant wind weather currents, and neither are impeded by any appreciable landforms. The result is a swirling cauldron of frequent bad weather, dangerous rogue waves, high winds, heavy snow and freezing sleet, often the result of warmer air meeting the colder air flowing off Antarctica. Conditions can blossom into polar cyclones, which ferociously circle the Southern Ocean unhindered. Striking unwary vessels with gale-force winds, they can quickly shred and blast sails out of their bolt ropes, as well

A Cape Horn souvenir patch. *From the Charles H. Lagerbom collection.*

as part or tangle rigging lines. Topmasts can easily snap off, crashing onto decks and men. Worse, entire sets of masts and rigging can be swept away in a situation known as dismasting.[21]

Thomaston native John Lermond wrote home to an aunt about such an occurrence from his time aboard the Maine-built sailing ship *S.D. Carleton.*

> *The word may reach you before this letter does, that the ship was dismantled on the other side of Cape Horn; that is, we lost top gallant, royal and sky sail masts and all the yards on them on the fore mast, the same on the main and the royal and sky sail mast on the mizzen. You look on the picture of the ship and imagine the four upper yards and two masts of the fore and main and two yards and a mast on the mizzen hanging and swinging about, and I think you can judge what kind of a mess we were in. I was on the watch on deck from four to eight, and I had been turned in one hour when the mate called me and told me that the masts were falling. The waves were washing over her, and you could not walk along the deck without holding on to something.*[22]

All hands spent the next two days working, except a man at the wheel and a lookout. It had not been a bad crossing.

> *The mate says we got around the horn very easy, as it was not very cold, and we did not get any heavy storms so as to have to run back. We have*

> *seen land but three times since we left.... The second island was Staten Land; we saw that for two days I think: there is a light-house there, no other people and high barren mountains, it must be very lonely there.... And then Cape Horn—I have seen that and am satisfied.... It looked very pretty at sundown that night.*[23]

At Penobscot Marine Museum, there is a ship model of *S.D. Carleton* that was made by a crew member who had doubled Cape Horn.

Ice could also be a problem. In the 1880s, Thomaston-built *Joseph Spinney* rounded Cape Horn in early December and found itself amid a tangle of ice. Altering course, it still sailed among icebergs for two thousand miles; the floes were miles long and one hundred feet high. Occasionally, they would thin out, but there were always two or three nearby. At its worst, the ice crowded in until the ship was almost completely surrounded. The *Joseph Spinney* took fifty days to clear it. Maine-built clipper *Red Jacket* encountered massive ice floes off the Horn, which is captured in a J.B. Smith & Son illustration. Its ice adventure was also immortalized on English ironstone dinnerware with a transfer image of *Red Jacket* battling Cape Horn ice. One plate is in the collection of the Maine Maritime Museum. *San Joaquin*, built in Freeport, collided with an iceberg that measured nine miles long. The collision partially dismasted the ship, stove in the bow and grounded them on the ice. The crew, working frantically through the night, was able to heave the ship off the floe.[24]

To further complicate matters, there is also False Cape Horn. On a map, the two places are not alike. Cape Horn is a high promontory on a small island, while False Cape Horn is a point of land off a large peninsula. False Cape Horn is thirty miles west of Cape Horn and seventeen miles north. For westbound vessels, False Cape Horn meant little, as they were already well to the south after passing true Cape Horn, at least below 56 degrees south. But for eastbound vessels coming from the Pacific, False Cape Horn posed a significant challenge, especially in bad weather and limited visibility. Mistakenly thinking they had passed the true Horn, a ship might veer northward too soon, right into Paso Franklin, the western approach to the Hermite and Wollaston Islands, twenty miles west of true Cape Horn.[25]

That fate fell on Damariscotta-built *Peri* in 1905. The 265-ton three-mast bark was eastbound when bad weather obscured visibility. A break in the storm allowed a quick glimpse of what officers thought was Cape Horn, but it proved to be False Cape Horn. When another weather break occurred, they saw land to their south where none should be, but they were too late

Right: A ship model of *S.D. Carleton* at Penobscot Marine Museum. *Photograph by Charles H. Lagerbom.*

Below: Rockland-built clipper ship *Red Jacket* among the ice floes off Cape Horn. *By J.B. Smith & Son, courtesy of the Library of Congress.*

in recognizing their predicament. With little room to maneuver, the captain ordered a lifeboat readied with provisions. They tried a starboard tack, but it was too late. Resuming their eastward course, they had no choice but to aim between the reefs and hope they might safely beach. To their surprise, *Peri* scraped through a narrow gap of kelp-covered reef and entered the waters east of Deceit Island, safely east of true Cape Horn. With no visibility, they had miraculously navigated through a narrow gap between Paso Franklin and Hermite Islands.[26]

The danger was not just at Cape Horn, but all along the way. Proceeding southward along eastern South America, the continent curls into the Atlantic. Cape Virgins, a prominent feature named by Magellan, marks the entrance to his strait. He reached it October 21, 1520, a feast day of Saint Ursula and the eleven thousand virgins. Magellan named it in Saint Ursula's honor. Over the years, steamers turned into these straits, while most sailing ships swung wide, skirting this dangerous expanse. The Falkland Islands, three hundred miles to the east, were handy if needed as refuge for repairs or more. Next, a stretch of water called LeMaire Strait separates the continent from Staten Island, both discovered and named by Schouten. Crews have described a phantom ship in this vicinity, referred to as the Ghost Ship of Cape Horn. It appears like a derelict vessel, with water washing its decks, a condition known as "half seas over." What is seen, appears like a vessel standing head on, pointing

The author testing water temperature in Straits of Magellan at Punta Arenas, Chile. *Photograph by Jon Cox, from the collection of Charles H. Lagerbom.*

southward, low in the water. Its sails look shortened, the whole vision very dark, as if its hull is black and sails are worn. The ghost ship clearly shows three masts and is higher on the fore than its main. However, once alongside, the illusion changes to a jumble of dangerous wet black rocks. Constant fog helped obscure the vision.

In 1907, a newspaper reported that the United States Hydrographic Office officially declared the Ghost Ship of Cape Horn nothing more than a rock, which, in bad weather or atmospheric irregularities, did appear to resemble a ship. Frequent sightings finally forced Argentina to investigate and found the apparition to be due to a strange freak of nature. Rock formations and cast shadows together looked very much like a bark under shortened sails. Authorities decided to mark charts starting five miles distant with, "Rock bearing the appearance of a ship." The Ghost Ship of Cape Horn was no more.[27]

In 1892–93, a young Thomaston woman was hired to be a teacher to the children of Captain and Mrs. Rivers aboard *A.G. Ropes*. Stonie Jameson kept a journal, *Around the Horn in 1892–1893*, and described their ordeal in the Strait of LeMaire.

> *Dec 13th: We are having a very hard time off the horn. Nothing but head winds and gales. Last Sat., we came through the Str. of Lemaire. It seemed so open that we should have a chance to go through, as we thought when we were way over there to the east so far, that, instead of going through the Str. of LeMaire, we should be forced around Falkland Island. We were over as far E. as 50 degrees—& the Str. Are in 65 degree…so you see, it was a great wonder we got there. We got neatly around Staten Land twice, and the wind howled and sent us way back to the north, and with all, we had 50 miles current in one 24 hours. I was so pleased to think we had a chance to go through, as it is rather pretty. You are so near the land & it is very high and plenty of snow on the mountain summits. It is a dangerous place to be in if the wind should happen to haul ahead or die out calm, as there is a strong current sitting on shore & not enough to make but short tack, yet it cuts off considerable distance, and they are always anxious to try if they possibly can to get through. It is 14 miles long through it and about 12 miles wide. So, you can see, with a good breeze, one can sail through it in a few hours. There was a long Eng. ship lost in there last year, and the crew took to their boats and went to St. John. But we have had no show since. SW gales & heavy sea is all we have had.*

Dec 18th: We are having it very rough today and for the days when I have not written. It would have been almost impossible to write. All we can do is sit still and read or talk. We have had a gale of wind lasting two days and a tremendous heavy sea on. She is pitching and rolling so that Pa cannot keep sail on her at all. We have a 10K breeze but so much sea on that we are making about 3 p. per hour, and the wind is so much ahead that we cannot get along at all. On one tack we NE—on the other SW—so you see how hard it is to get to the west.

Dec 20th: This has been a very exciting day and one I do not wish to go through again but shall probably have to. A furious gale came on this morning about 1 o'clock and threatened to do considerable damage, as the sea was tremendous. She was rolling herself full every sea, and Pa was expecting any moment when one of the masts, if not all of them, would snap off. About 3:30 o'clock, the gale was at its height when a sea struck just at the break of the poop and smashing in the mate's window—thick sea plate glass—too, tore off the shutter…inside filling his room full & flooding the forward cabin so that steward & Clarence dished up 10 large buckets of water. Some reached as far aft as Lena's window & came in round that & wet her bed all over—but did no damage there. Smashed the mate's chair, tore down his bookcase demolishing his clock watch and everything else that was within its reach. I found one of his stockings way in the after cabin, where the sea washed it in. You can't imagine what a noise the water makes when it strikes. I thought all the spars was coming down sure. We had had sea strike her before but not anything like that. It is the first time they have had a window smashed in on this ship. It tooked [sic] *the stove funnel off, & one of the men just jumped in time to save it. One man was washed some distance on the main deck but not hurt seriously. Fortunately, there was no one at the break of the poop when it struck, or they would have been washed overboard sure. Altogether, it was quite a time, and I do not wish it to occur many more times. We had a strong gale all the rest of the day, but by night, the wind had spent its force some, and we were little more comfortable.*[28]

After the LeMaire Strait, Beagle Channel runs between Tierra del Fuego and Navarino Island, offering a potential but difficult westward route. Optional passages are found around the Wollaston and Hermite Islands to the north of Cape Horn. They all present their own challenges, with treacherous winds and narrow sea lanes, a significant risk of getting driven onto rocks. Wide-open Drake Passage, south of the Horn, provides

The author on the bridge while in the Beagle Channel. *From the Charles H. Lagerbom collection.*

plenty of sea room to maneuver amid constant wind changes. Even with extreme waves, this route was most favored. Ships tried their luck through the LeMaire Strait or swung far eastward, avoiding Staten Island completely, before they began their battle to make westing. Approaching the Horn, islands to the north on the starboard side might be glimpsed in decent weather. If a vessel did not make enough distance south, Lennox and Neuva Islands and even bits of rock named Evout Island or Barnevelt Island could rear up out of mist and waves. The aptly named Isles of Deceit come next, fingers of rocky outcrops trailing down into Drake Passage, appropriately situated to catch unwary navigators. Finally, there comes Cape Horn itself, a couple of miles south of the Hermite Island group. Once beyond the Horn, the way to the north and west is open.

2

ATTEMPTS

There was an old man of Cape Horn who wished he had never been born.
—Edward Lear

The dangerous and grueling Cape Horn route has long been recognized as the main way to get around the American continents. Even with its treacherous waters, it became a popular route for Americans starting in the late eighteenth century. The American flag was first taken around Cape Horn in 1788. It was carried by a little 90-ton Massachusetts-built sloop named *Lady Washington* in an attempt to test the efficacy of a Cape Horn route to obtain California seal hides, which would then be taken on to China for trade. The attempt was successful, and *Lady Washington* and the larger 230-ton *Columbia Redivivia* solved the China trade riddle. They also blazed a path for American ships to double Cape Horn. It was not long before Nantucket whaleships followed, including *Beaver* in 1791.[29]

Once established, the Cape Horn route became defined by time. How long it took to go this way varied widely, often taking much longer than planned. Only twenty-two clipper ship passages westbound from an Atlantic port around Cape Horn are on record as having made it in less than one hundred days. By far, more took longer, posting an average of eighteen or more days just to double the Horn. Most took over three weeks to double it, primarily because the dangerous route included the polar environment of the extreme Southern Ocean. William Armstrong Fairburn compared the

average doubling times of eighty-two clipper ships that made at least five westward passages around Cape Horn, mostly from 1850 to 1860 and the following decade. He found that most encountered heavy weather and slow progress, including eight clippers that had been built in Maine.[30]

So, why voyage there to do battle with Cape Horn waters? It had to do with speed and need for it, which dramatically increased after America's War of 1812. The United States was growing increasingly wealthy, and it "would not long endure the risks and discomforts of the antiquated method of ocean transportation." There was a growing demand for goods as America's interior opened for settlement and development. This, coupled with increased European immigration, spurred the demand for imported goods, as well as faster, reliable transoceanic capabilities. Results included the establishment of a regular ship service between New York and Liverpool, like the Black Ball Line of transport packets. The newer, faster ships used in this service were naturally considered for other new routes, such as the China Trade and the California Run. The longer, safer route had been around Africa's southern tip, the Cape of Good Hope. To get to the American West Coast or China more quickly, one had to go around Cape Horn.[31]

Thus, in a curious confluence of economics, ship design, market forces and changing demographics, the American clipper ship was created. East Coast shipyards, including those in Maine, were eager to produce the requisite vessels and named them accordingly in hopes of illustrating their speed, power and range. Historian Samuel Eliot Morison wrote, "For centuries, shipbuilders had maintained that you could have either speed or burden, but not both; but New York and Boston wanted both, and they got it." Over sixty clipper ships were constructed in Maine shipyards, about 15 percent of the total American fleet. Another source puts the number at ninety.[32]

Before the arrival of clipper ships, Maine connections with Cape Horn include the 1800 Kennebunk-built *Atahualpa*. Engaged in the Asia trade, the vessel regularly went by way of Cape Horn and the rigorous Northwest route. Other ships sailed that route for China, including the *Massachusetts* under Captain Amassa Delano of Duxbury, Massachusetts. His crew for the 1790 voyage included a carpenter's mate named Elias Parkman, who later resided on Maine's Penobscot River. He may have influenced a young neighbor named William Lowder, born 1785 in Castine. Lowder became a shipwright and ship captain. But early in life, he went whaling, rounded Cape Horn and pioneered routes into Pacific waters. Parkman may have introduced him to the industry. New England whalers had

been making multiyear voyages there since 1791. Another possible link was wealthy Bostonian and Lowder in-law Benjamin Bussey. He bought a house on Boston's Hawley Street that was once owned by Joseph Barrell. With others, including Bussey, Barrell outfitted Boston's first vessels to sail around Cape Horn.[33]

Obed Paddock was a Nantucket-born whaling captain who retired to Maine. Born on November 6, 1762, he sailed *Olive Branch* from 1797 to 1799 and rounded Cape Horn to reach Pacific hunting grounds off Chile. They returned with 1,100 barrels of oil, all but 100 from sperm whales. Paddock married Margaret Macy and retired to Fairfield, Maine, in 1800. In failing health, he became housebound for his last thirteen years. A devout Quaker, he died on January 10, 1834. Charles F. Coffin, another Nantucket-born whaling captain who retired to Maine, was born on April 18, 1794. He married Mary Folsom and made one whaling voyage from Nantucket in 1836 as master of the *Washington*. They rounded Cape Horn, but Coffin left the ship, replaced by Stephen Bailey. Coffin died in Maine on December 19, 1873. Maine native Benjamin C. Gardner became a Nantucket whaling captain and made two voyages around Cape Horn. Louise Sturtevant, his wife, accompanied him both trips. In January 1826, he sailed the 1810-built whaleship *Martha* to Pacific waters and returned in April 1828 with 1,843 barrels of sperm whale oil.[34]

In 1834, Wiscasset conducted its own whaling venture with the 380-ton *Wiscasset*, built in Maine in 1833. Sailing down the Sheepscot River on May 13, 1834, they headed for Cape Horn and Pacific waters. Off the Horn in a terrible storm, *Wiscasset*'s rudder was damaged. They were able to effect repairs. When spotted off the coast of New Zealand in April 1836, a whaler reported they had already taken in 1,350 barrels of whale oil. The Nobleboro-built 111-ton schooner *Tyleston* made thirteen whaling voyages starting in 1839. Its career totals included 756 barrels of oil, 616 of them from sperm whales. Some voyages came back empty or with fewer than 25 barrels; one voyage brought back only 6. In 1854, on its last whaling voyage, the whaler managed to get to Cape Horn, only to encounter gales so severe that they strained the ship. *Tyleston* returned to Pernambuco in Brazil, where the worn-out vessel was condemned.[35]

Maine native David Densmore of China went into whaling in 1841. At twenty-eight, he became the captain of the *Massasoit* with a motley crew of thirty-four either drunken or greenhand sailors. Most were foreign, and some came from Densmore's hometown, including his brother who was first mate and his cousin who was third mate. Another brother and cousin

signed on as seamen. Three weeks out, Densmore faced a potential mutiny from his crew, as they were unwilling to face Cape Horn. He grabbed a pistol, called all hands on deck and gave what he later termed a "stump speech." Promising dire consequences for any insubordination, he dared any man to speak. Either the speech worked or he had misunderstood the rumblings, as *Massasoit*'s crew offered no resistance to orders, and they successfully fought their way around Cape Horn. Densmore published his autobiography forty years later.[36]

Isle au Haut native Abel Douglass was born in 1841. He was eight years old when he traveled with his family to San Francisco by way of Cape Horn in 1849 as part of the California gold rush. By the 1860s, he and brother Albert had migrated to Victoria, Canada, and started a whaling business with partner James Dawson. They founded Whaletown in 1869 on Cortes Island, just off British Columbia. Douglass died in 1907 and was buried at Lake View Cemetery in Seattle.[37]

Maine-built whaler *Henry Kneeland* reached Cape Horn while homeward bound in the first week of January 1854. Enoch Carter Cloud kept a journal and wrote:

> *We were carrying every stitch of canvass which we could spread, when we were struck by a terrific snow squall, which threatened to relieve us of our masts! I went up to assist in furling the main-top-gallant-sail, got it furled and found I could not get down! My hands were frozen stiff, and I could not take hold of the shrouds. I laid across the to'gallant yard and beat my hands with all my force, in order to start the circulation of the blood. Could not do it! Things began to get desperate! My clothes were freezing, and such was the pain which I was suffering that I really began to feel unconcerned whether I got safely to the deck or fell a mangled corpse! Winding my arms and legs around the shrouds, I commenced a very perilous descent, not knowing or caring whether I got safely down or not! I managed, at length, to reach the deck and at once, plunged my hands into a tub of cold water. A short time sufficed to bring them to, and then I suffered!! I never felt such pain before, and I am quite sure that I am not very anxious to experience the like again!*[38]

Henry Kneeland had to navigate around numerous icebergs as it rounded the Horn. It finally arrived at New Bedford in April 1854 with 3,386 barrels of oil, 222 of them from sperm whales, and nearly eighteen tons of baleen. Steam-converted 313-ton *Lucretia* was an 1877 Bath-built Goss & Sawyer bark that made ten voyages to North Pacific waters. *Lucretia*

proved a slow sailor and was unlucky as well, barely surviving a hurricane off Bermuda on its refitted maiden voyage. It lost its topmasts, bowsprit, numerous spars and all boats but one. After repairs, it tried to round Cape Horn, but adverse winds forced it to instead take the Indian Ocean route. *Lucretia* arrived in San Francisco in November 1882 and missed the entire Arctic whaling season. It later became a San Francisco shanghaier.[39]

Maine native Leander C. Owen of Brownfield moved to New Bedford as a young man. At fifteen, he went into whaling, spending the next forty years in the industry. As captain, he made at least six east-to-west doublings of Cape Horn. Later in his career, he worked out of San Francisco. In 1886, he brought the whaler *Mary and Susan* back around Cape Horn to New Bedford with 750 barrels of oil and 17,000 pounds of baleen. Leander C. Owen died on March 25, 1911, at the age of seventy-seven and was buried at Oak Grove Cemetery in Tisbury, Massachusetts.[40]

This growing need for vessels to double Cape Horn translated into the construction of better, faster and sturdier cargo-carrying ships. By late 1840s, Maine shipbuilders entered one of the more exciting eras in their maritime history. Samuel Morison called it the greatest revolution in naval architecture since the days of Hawkins and Drake.[41] The clipper ship period lasted only a few years and vanished with the American Civil War, but it produced such a glorious era that it still stirs the imagination and conjures up dramatic and picturesque visions of long, sleek ships sailing away on the wind, festooned with yards of white billowing canvas. It has embedded itself into the American consciousness and character, much like the iconic American cowboy. Part of that character meant testing a ship, its crew's skills and their stamina in Cape Horn waters.

Flying Scud was an extreme clipper ship built in Damariscotta in 1853 by Metcalf & Norris, and it was sold to New York owners the following year for $100,000. The vessel was 221 feet long and weighed 1,713 tons, twice the size of the average clipper. *Flying Scud* sported seventeen sails and required a skilled crew to handle all of that canvas. For a heavy merchant ship, it was considered quite fast; once, it logged 4,620 nautical miles in sixteen days for an average run of 288 miles per day. In one day alone, it claimed the fastest run ever, traveling 449 miles in a twenty-four-hour period. *Flying Scud*'s first Cape Horn run from New York to San Francisco in 1862, however, was a disappointment. The voyage took 188 days, as it was delayed by storms and damage, much of it suffered off Cape Horn. The following year, the clipper was sold to English owners and renamed *Cestrian*. It was still operating in 1871, then under Liverpool ownership.[42]

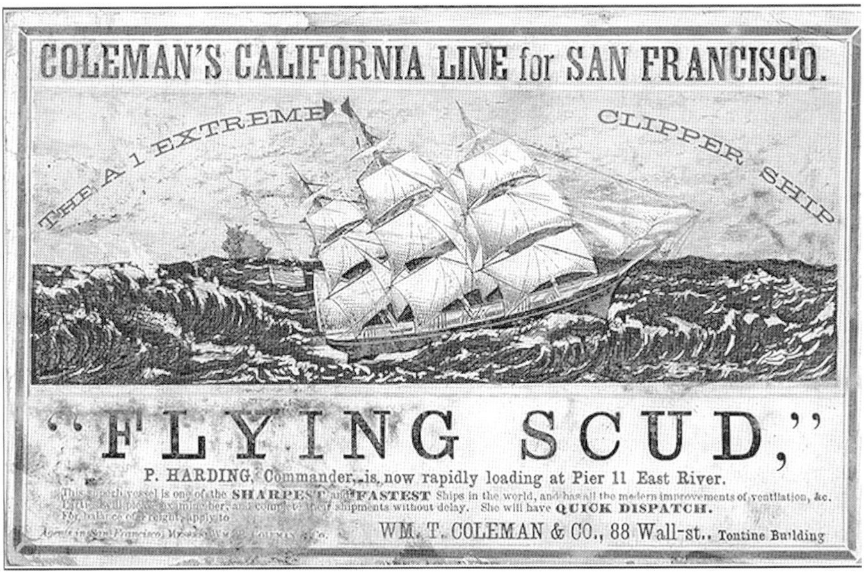

Flying Scud, color woodcut, Nesbitt and Company New York, circa 1855. *From* Westward by Sea: A Maritime Perspective on American Expansion 1820–1890, *Library of Congress*.

Another Damariscotta-built clipper operated for years. *North American* was built in 1851 in Damariscotta by Algernon Austin. It was 194 feet long, 38 feet in beam and 28 feet deep. The ship was used to transport immigrants during the gold rush and the American Civil War, doubling Cape Horn on numerous runs to the West Coast. It then went through a series of name changes, including *Marianna VI* and *Philadelphia*, until finally named *Redemptora* in 1888. Its last name was in honor of Brazil's Princess Isabel, who abolished slavery that year. The clipper was used as a coal hulk until it was abandoned in 1898 on the shores of western Australia.[43]

Doubling Cape Horn was difficult enough, yet some voyages were made even more challenging by brutal or cruel captains and mates. One of the more infamous Horn voyages occurred on the Maine-built Sewall ship *Matterhorn* in the late 1860s. Harpswell captain Peleg Curtis, due to be its master, backed out at the last minute with an ailing wife. Due to a captain shortage, he was replaced for the voyage to Callao by William Frazier, who had been the first mate on another Sewall ship. As mate, Frazier reportedly killed a sailor on Christmas Day after he allegedly refused to turn-to on the holiday. When the man objected to being put in irons for his transgression, Frazier hit him in the head with a capstan bar, and he died a few hours later.[44] Upon *Matterhorn*'s arrival at Callao, Frazier reported that all was

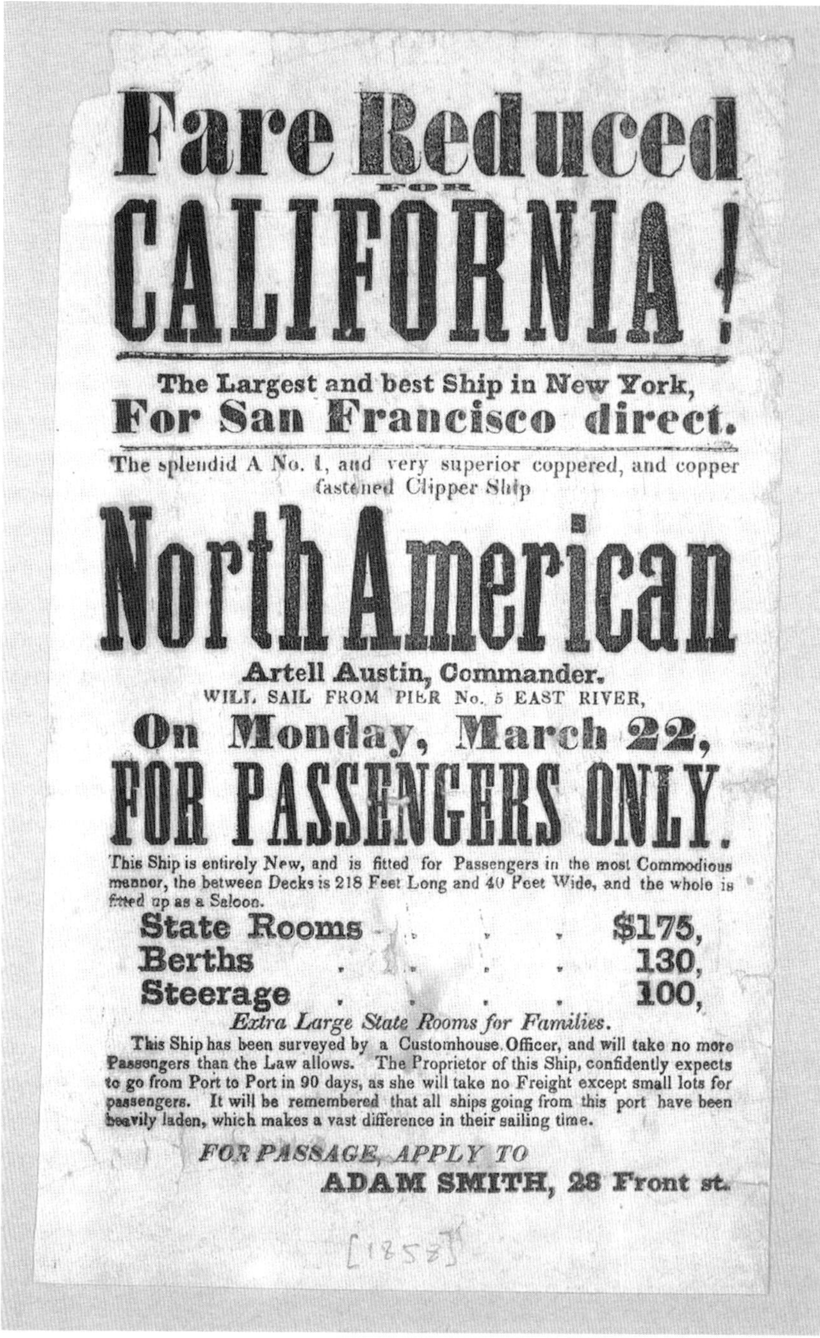

Clipper Ship *North American* to sail for California, 1852. *Calisphere, public domain.*

well. Reports soon surfaced, however, that two sailors had been killed off Cape Horn. The first mate, Bowdoin-native Zaccheus Allen, was sent to San Francisco to stand trial for cruel treatment of the crew. A murder charge was later added. Allen had had trouble with sailor Moses Blake as the ship battled its way off Cape Horn. Allen testified:

> *I ordered Blake on deck; he got up on his feet but did not start to go out. I then put my hand on his shoulder and gave him a push when he said, "Don't you put your hands on me," and then said if I put my hand on him, he would "cut my guts out," and put his hand behind him as though was going to draw his knife.*[45]

Allen grabbed a capstan bar, and a fight ensued. Blake jumped into the forecastle to avoid the blows and refused to come out. The mate got a revolver and met Blake near the main hatch, at which point Blake pulled a knife and jumped at him. Allen fired twice, as did Captain Frazier, who had arrived with his own pistol. Blake dropped to the deck, was hung in irons for an hour and then was let down to have his wounds tended. He was kept on top of the after house, except for meals, and at night, he was put down in the lazaret, the low space beneath the after part of the main deck, usually used as storeroom. By December 31, Blake was missing and assumed to have jumped overboard. A sailor reported that Blake and Alfred Morris had made plans to take over the ship. Allen also had difficulty with one of the German crew members aboard. He had also refused orders while the *Matterhorn* was off Cape Horn. Allen knocked the man to the deck, and then the man raced into the forecastle and emerged with a large stick. Allen promptly beat him with his fists. When the German grabbed a belaying pin, Allen deftly took it from him and beat him over the head with it.[46]

Matterhorn's steward Emanuel had also been disciplined for using a dirty bucket to draw drinking water. When he denied doing it, Allen grabbed and choked him. Captain Frazier had to restrain the enraged steward when he later emerged on deck with a carving knife. Later, Emanuel left the cabin with a dish but went overboard. *Matterhorn* backed the yards as soon as it could, but he was never found. Alfred Morris, a Maine native, later testified that Allen and Frazier had done more than just hang Moses Blake in irons. They beat the sailor with a small iron block and rope until his face was so swollen, the sailor could hardly see. Morris testified that Frazier then said to kill Blake. Others echoed the testimony and added that the steward had also been beaten around the face with brass knuckles. The Sewall Company

defended their captain and used its considerable resources; first mate Allen was acquitted of all charges.[47]

Cape Horn could also bring out the best in tough characters. Captain Daniel Smith Goodell Jr. was born on February 16, 1853, in Searsport. In June 1876, aboard *Brown Brothers* in a furious storm off Cape Horn, he rescued William W. Beach. The sailor had been swept over the side by a wave. Goodell affixed a rope around himself and jumped overboard after him. He was awarded a medal from the Massachusetts Humane Society. On September 20, 1890, however, Goodell pleaded no contest in Boston district court for restraining and flogging one of his crew members. He was fined $350. Goodell retired from the sea in 1895. On the 1874 Bath-built 1,509-ton *Gatherer*, the crew was so brutalized that one sailor reportedly jumped off the royal yard into Cape Horn waters rather than endure the physical beatings by the mates and captain. Another sailor committed suicide that same voyage, while a third was shot by the mate. When *Edward O'Brien II* began to leak off Cape Horn, its crew was ordered to the pumps. Sailors later complained that even after the danger had passed, the mates kept them at it, all the while subjecting them to abuse with no relief in wet, stormy conditions.[48]

The Bath-built medium clipper ship *Carrier Pigeon* was launched in 1852 and measured 175.5 feet in length. With its distinctive carved figurehead of its namesake, the clipper departed Boston January 28, 1853, for San Francisco on its maiden voyage. The ship and cargo were insured for $195,000. *Carrier Pigeon* had little difficulty doubling Cape Horn but ran aground in fog off San Francisco. It wrecked only 500 feet from shore although everyone survived. The June 10, 1853 issue of the *Daily Alta California* reported, "Her bows lay about 500 feet from the beach, and she rests amidships on a ledge of rocks, which have broken the ship's back. The tide ebbs and flows in her and is up to her between-decks."[49] In 1871, Pigeon Point Lighthouse was built where the clipper had wrecked.

While transporting general cargo from Boston to the West Coast, the Maine-built clipper *Noonday* had little trouble as it literally flew around Cape Horn, only to strike an uncharted rock just miles from its final destination. On January 1, 1863, approximately eight miles off North Farallon Island, just outside San Francisco Bay, *Noonday* bounced off the rock with no visible damage. In reality, the hull had been stove in and quickly filled with water. Captain and crew took to boats and *Noonday* sank in forty fathoms. A nearby pilot boat named *Relief* saved everyone. On charts, the rock was eventually marked and named Noonday Rock.[50]

Searsport native and Cape Horn captain Daniel Smith Goodell Jr. *Courtesy of the Penobscot Marine Museum.*

The 1,371-ton medium clipper *Mary Robinson*, built in 1854 at Trufant & Drummond Shipyard in Bath, measured 215 feet by 38.6 feet by 22.6 feet. It made six Cape Horn westbound voyages to San Francisco. On its maiden Horn voyage, *Mary Robinson* spent an entire month trying to double it in the face of "heavy gales and continual snowstorms." In 1864, it ran its fastest time in 115 days. On that voyage, the ship was in sight of another clipper, *Carrier Dove*, off of Cape Horn and ended up beating them to San Francisco by 18 days. With 1,300 tons of guano aboard, *Mary Robinson* was lost on June 27, 1864, at Howland's Island in the Pacific.[51]

The January 1872 issue of Belfast's *Republican Journal* reported the Bucksport death of seafarer Captain John Odom. Back in 1808, Odom's first ship had wrecked in northern waters of the Baltic Sea. He survived and spent the next half century transiting the world. As a deep-water captain, Odom is credited with crossing the Atlantic forty-three times, as well as multiple doublings of Cape Horn. The barkentine *Holliswood*

was built in Massachusetts in 1893 and was in San Francisco when it was purchased by the Pendleton maritime family of Maine. They sent Islesboro native Captain George Alden Warren to bring it back east. Warren and the *Holliswood* encountered hurricane conditions off southern Chile, which dismasted the ship, necessitating a port visit for repairs. Continuing to Cape Horn, the *Holliswood* encountered severe weather that necessitated more repairs. The *Holliswood* then worked the East Coast, eventually lost with all hands on a voyage to South America.[52]

Maine native Captain Rasmus B. Anderson saw his ship *Alaska* catch fire off Cape Horn. He ran the vessel ashore, intentionally sinking it at Orange Bay, which doused the flames. He then pumped it out, refloated the vessel and continued on his way. Searsport resident Captain Albert Nickels Blanchard had been born at sea and had many Cape Horn adventures. While in command of the bark *Herbert Black*, it lost its rudder in a ferocious storm in the far South Atlantic. Blanchard constructed a jury rudder, which allowed them to successfully double the Horn with improvised steering gear. The ship visited its ports and returned back around Cape Horn on its homeward voyage, still with a jury-rigged rudder. Without further repairs, *Herbert Black* completed its entire voyage all the way to New York, a feat many consider to have never been equaled. One account says scars on its planking from the chains of the jury-rigged rudder were visible for years.[53]

3
GOLD FEVER

Whatever you do, make westing—make westing!
—sailing directions for Cape Horn

Maine's connection with Cape Horn dramatically expanded after 1848, when gold was discovered at Sutter's Mill on the American River north of San Francisco. A massive wave of gold fever washed to the U.S. East Coast, causing many Mainers and Maine-built ships to try their luck on a Cape Horn voyage. Most forty-niners who headed west to the gold fields went by sea, as did most of the mining equipment, lumber, supplies and hardware. In 1849, a total of 775 ships brought more than forty thousand people and tons of materials to San Francisco. Known as gold rush ships, more than five hundred vessels arrived in the last half of the year; less than a dozen had arrived in all of 1848. By end of 1849, numerous brigs, barks and schooners had left Maine for California—thirteen from Bangor alone. Three sailed from Belfast, Maine, and the state's governor even said farewell at one departure.[54]

Belfast earned a place in California gold rush history by being the starting point of one of the first voyages to the West Coast for the gold fields. During the fall of 1848, once rumors were confirmed, gold rush fever reached the town. Belfast shipbuilder Asa Faunce was finishing the construction of a 212-ton bark named *Suliote*. It was 105 feet long, drew 11 feet and could carry a decent amount of cargo and passengers. Faunce immediately made it available to take paying passengers to California

to seek their fortunes. *Suliote* was to sail at the end of January under Captain Josiah Simpson. The schooner *Eudorus*, under Captain Charles L. Wiggin, would sail two weeks later from Frankfort. There was no shortage of interested participants. Fifty area men, mostly in their early twenties, raced to secure a berth aboard *Suliote*, willingly paying up to $150 per fare. Twenty-four hailed from Bangor, including three-fourths of the town's Bangor Quartette. Apparently, gold fever was enough to break up the group, two of whom, Alonzo Wiggin and Robert Cram, departed on *Suliote*, while the third, Rufus Wiggin, left on *Eudorus*. Only Renaldo Wiggin opted to stay in Bangor.[55]

For many, it was the opportunity of a lifetime. The Belfast men who took this journey included Thomas Farrow, Curtis Merrill, William L. Torry, Freeman Patterson and Benjamin Griffin, a recent editor of the *Belfast Republican* newspaper. Torry returned to Maine after holding numerous public positions in California. He died in Rockland at the age of sixty-four in 1883. Camden gold seekers included George T. Crabtree, Joseph Cusack, Joseph P. Dyer and Fisher H. Follansbee. Crabtree did not linger long out west, as he returned to Rockland and married Clementine McLoon in 1852. Another *Suliote* passenger was Thomas Dinsmore of China, who was interviewed years later in 1915 about the voyage, when he was ninety-three years old. On January 21, 1849, many of the excited passengers filed into Bangor's Hammond Street Church to hear specially

Advertisement for upcoming *Suliote* voyage to California. *Courtesy of the Belfast Historical Society and Museum.*

prepared sermons by Reverends George Shepard and S.L. Caldwell. The bark was launched on January 30, 1849. Loading for California began at once; the pace was frantic. Soon, everyone was aboard. The *Suliote* became the first vessel to sail from Maine for the California gold rush.[56]

The passage was not a quick one; overall, the distance was sixteen thousand miles. Thirty-three days into the voyage, the ship neared the equator. The *Suliote* arrived in Rio de Janeiro on March 19, then sailed the following day. So fast was the turn-around that no letters from passengers were posted. There was no time to delay—California awaited. In addition, the ship and its crew were entering waters in the southern hemisphere's late fall months. On April 16, 1850, the *Suliote* encountered bad weather off of Cape Horn. An artist named K. Johnson later painted a watercolor of the *Suliote* battling its way through heavy seas off the Horn. No other information has been found as to the artist or when the painting was made. One clue might be the presence of a Maine passenger aboard the *Suliote* named Aaron H. Johnson of Stillwater, perhaps the artist's relation. The auction information reported that the watercolor was purchased in New England.[57]

The *Suliote* was off of Cape Horn when tragedy struck. On a pitch-black night with a heavy sea running, Captain Josiah Simpson's eighteen-year-old son, Edwin Paul Simpson, stood near the ship's wheel. The *Suliote* gave a sudden lurch in the rough seas. The wet deck provided no purchase, and Simpson was hurled overboard into frothing water. Captain Simpson's cry of "Edwin is overboard!" roused the crew, but nothing could be done. In such seas, a lowered boat would be swamped as soon as it hit the water. Passengers and crew helplessly watched in horror as Edwin, a favorite of everyone, floated farther and farther behind with each successive wave. Howling winds covered any sound.[58]

On May 10, the battered ship limped into Valparaiso, Chile. A passenger named Griffin, either William or Benjamin, posted a letter that was written on April 23 about Captain Simpson losing his son off Cape Horn. He wrote that the tragedy destroyed all that may have been termed the pleasure of the voyage and that it had clouded everyone's experience the rest of the trip. Griffin also noted he needed to wear three pairs of pants, woolen shirts and three coats to ward off Cape Horn cold. For two weeks, they rested at Valparaiso while the storm-damaged vessel was repaired, and then they sailed on for California. The *Suliote* arrived in San Francisco July 20, 1849, after 171 days—not a record-breaking passage. The *Suliote*'s voyage, coupled with loss of his son, ended Captain Simpson's days at sea. He returned to

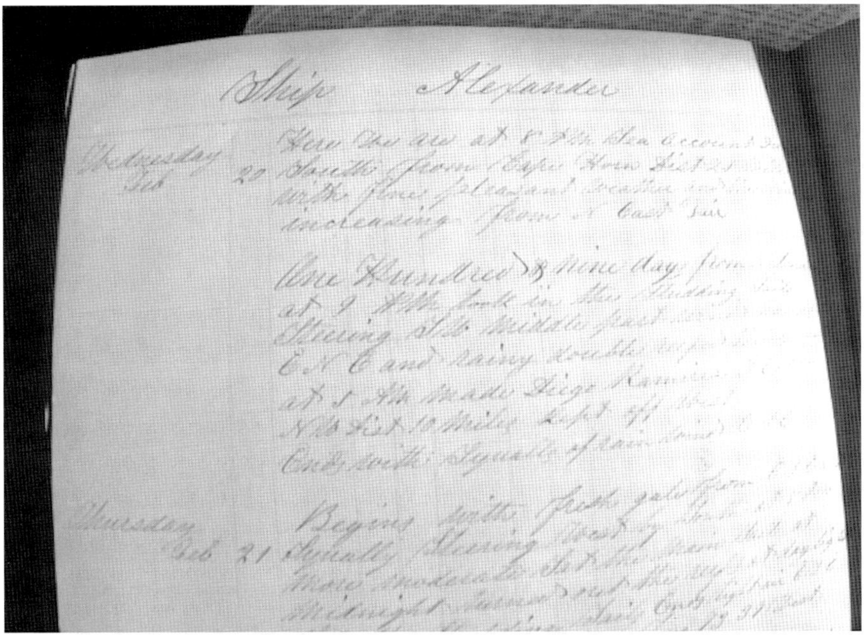

Logbook of the ship *Alexander* while it was off Cape Horn. *Photograph by Charles H. Lagerbom, from the Penobscot Marine Museum.*

Belfast and built Simpson's Wharf, where he engaged in commerce. The wharf burned in 1873.[59]

A logbook for the ship *Alexander* survives in the Penobscot Marine Museum. The captain used the heading "Bound for California" on its 1849 voyage. Rounding Cape Horn in February, it encountered difficult weather. The logbook account for Wednesday, February 20, starts with the words "here we are."

For many Maine vessels as well as Mainers, the Cape Horn route was a one-way, one-time passage to California. Once there, most ships were abandoned, as crews themselves deserted to test their luck in the gold fields. As empty ships piled up in the harbor, they became known as "Rotten Row." Some vessels never arrived. After surviving its Cape Horn voyage and depositing gold seekers on the West Coast, the brig *San Jacinto* was lost off Humboldt Bar, California, in 1851. It had been built in Belfast in 1846.[60]

The 147-ton Lubec-built schooner *Mary Stuart* was launched in 1846. Two years later, it sailed from New York to California and never returned from the West Coast. In 1849, two years after the Whiting-built 157-

ton brigantine *Quoddy Belle* was launched, it loaded people from Lubec who were also desperate to reach the California gold fields. The *Quoddy Belle* rounded Cape Horn and was later wrecked on the Pacific side of Panama. It was eventually purchased by San Francisco owners. The town of Whiting also produced the bark *Ada*, which sailed for California on September 10, 1849. It reached San Francisco the following April after a turbulent Cape Horn doubling, another vessel never to return east. The *Alfonzo* was a 212-ton brig that was built in 1850 in Pembroke; it barely survived its only Cape Horn passage and finished out its service in the Australia trade in 1854.[61]

In 1848, Eastport built the 128-ton schooner *Banner* expressly for the gold fields. That same year, the town launched the 113-ton steamer *S.B. Wheeler*. Not intended to make its own way around Cape Horn, the plan was for the steamer to be carried around the Horn aboard the bark *Fanny*, which was also built in Eastport. The *Fanny* was launched that July and then intentionally sunk so that *S.B. Wheeler* could be floated over it. The bark was then raised with the steamer on it and loaded with cargo. When enough paying passengers arrived, the ships departed for San Francisco. The two ships arrived on April 1, 1851, after a perilous voyage in which the *Fanny* had been struck by lightning three different times. The overloaded bark struggled in Cape Horn waters, but luckily, the weather cooperated, and they successfully doubled it. The steamer *S.B. Wheeler* worked on the Sacramento River for years and even made a voyage to Honolulu, Hawaii, in 1854.[62]

The Thomaston-built *Algoma* was a 293-ton ship launched in 1845. It departed Baltimore on March 1, 1849, with fifty-six passengers and a twelve-man crew and arrived San Francisco on September 26, 1849. It suffered a dreadful Cape Horn passage. The *Algoma* was then used in the Panama trade. The bark *Condor* departed Portland for California on August 20, 1848. It was so buffeted by constant gales off Cape Horn that it took the crew thirty-five days to double. In 1847, the Perry-built 135-ton brig *Amelia* was launched. It sailed for California before returning to Maine with a Cape Horn passage described as "simply awful." The 138-ton brig *B.M. Prescott* was built in Robbinston in 1848 and sailed for California, but it never made it, as it went ashore at Gull Island. Robbinston also launched the 604-ton ship *Brewer* in 1848, which was also bound for the gold fields. In December 1850, after severe Cape Horn storms, the leaking *Brewer* arrived at Valparaiso. It was eventually sold in 1866 and renamed *Atlantic*. The first Sewall-built ship of Bath to

double the Horn was the *Roger Sherman.* It sailed from Antwerp to San Francisco in July 1849 and arrived in May 1850. Built in 1835, the *Roger Sherman* was then considered old and strained. Not worth sending back to Maine, it was immediately sold for $5,000.[63]

In 1847, Leeds native Captain Lebbeus Curtis II sailed the bark *Solomon Piper* through the Straits of LeMaire, bound for California. A very religious Mainer, he was known to note in his logbook upon the completion of any daring maneuver the words, "By the Grace of God, we came through." By 1850, when the California Gold Rush was in full throttle, Curtis left Searsport to seek his fortune in California. That voyage took 148 days. Searsport captain Elijah Cyphers was born in 1806. He married Rebecca B. Stimpson and had five daughters and a son. When gold fever hit Waldo County, Cyphers left it all behind and went west to the gold fields. He was never heard from again. On the other hand, in the early 1850s, Searsport captain Richard Emery Patterson went to California and then on to Colorado, where he struck it rich. He returned home to Searsport in 1864.[64]

The Robbinston-built 300-ton barkentine *Carbon* was launched in 1851. It suffered dreadful damage while rounding Cape Horn that year and returned to Boston in 1853. The *Carbon* was dismasted on the homeward passage. The Warren-built 314-ton *Midas* was launched in 1849 and barely survived its maiden Horn passage, only to arrive in San Francisco during an outbreak of cholera. Addison was the hometown of Mainer Nathaniel N. Wass, a ship's carpenter at Addison Point Shipyard. His specialty was making spars. But in 1849, he caught gold fever and departed with other locals on bark *Belgrade* around Cape Horn to San Francisco. It is not clear if anyone found their fortune, but Nathaniel returned to Addison and continued working in the shipyards.[65]

At least five Waldoboro-built ships were contracted for a gold rush California voyage. The 200-ton brig *Antares* left Massachusetts in September 1849 with seven passengers and reached San Francisco after 152 days. Another was the 1836-built 800-ton *Caroline Clark*, which transported thirty-eight passengers in 190 days. They were delayed for weeks off of Cape Horn. The *Caroline Clark* left that November and reached the West Coast on June 14, 1850, never to sail the East Coast again. The 299-ton 1845-built bark *Louisiana* delivered forty Philadelphia passengers in 161 days; it also ended its days on the West Coast. The 164-ton schooner *Pedomonte* took eight passengers from New Orleans but had to put in at both Rio de Janeiro to prepare for its Horn passage as well as Valparaiso afterward to affect repairs. Waldoboro shipbuilder Edwin Achorn built

at least four clipper ships for the California gold rush. The 1,091-ton *Woodcock* enjoyed a fair, if somewhat mundane, career; all of its Cape Horn doublings were decent, if uneventful, a notable achievement in itself. The *Woodcock* was eventually bilged when it was wrecked off Dungeness, Ireland. Another was the *Wings of the Morning*, which had back-to-back westward New York–San Francisco runs of 165 and 145 days, the former of which was delayed by incessant headwinds. It also endured a heavy gale just 5 days out, which carried away its jib-boom and flying jib-boom, all three topgallant masts and the slings and truss of its main yard. Its skylight was stove in, and its decking was damaged as well. The *Wings of the Morning* was sent to Rio de Janeiro for repairs, then lost its jib-boom for the second time after three weeks of nasty weather and heavy gales off of Cape Horn. There, its head rails and part of its stern moldings were carried away. On an eastbound passage, the *Wings of the Morning* lost its topmast and had to be sent to Rio de Janeiro for repairs. On another westward Cape Horn passage, the ship carried a load of lumber and mining supplies for some Waldoboro prospectors. Built in 1852, the *Wings of the Morning* finished its career working in the Pacific.[66]

Between April 1849 and April 1850, sixty-two thousand potential miners, known as forty-niners, arrived in San Francisco by way of Cape Horn. Good money could be made by transporting them west or perhaps shipping the equipment they desperately needed. One Thomaston bark was sold in New York City for $26,000. The new owner announced that its destination was California and filled the vessel with paying passengers in less than a week. Desperate to get to the gold fields and strike it rich, they happily paid up to $200 per person. The owner then filled the bark with $50,000 worth of cargo, mostly items that were in great demand, such as picks and shovels. Fortunes could be made in this California gold rush, not necessarily just by those who were going to dig for gold.[67]

4
GLORY DAYS

Well, she had us sort of hypnotized,
No time to catch our breath.
If you want to love your life, well you have to flirt with death.
Sail close to the harnessed wind and treat all risks with scorn.
A farm boy and an unyoked team
Ploughed their way around the wild Cape Horn.
—lyrics from "Around the Wild Cape Horn"

The glory days of rounding Cape Horn came with the clipper ship, many of which were built in Maine, and their later cousin, the roomier cargo carriers known as down-easters. By the 1850s, the passage around Cape Horn had become a regular feature for a California voyage, akin to the times spent in the doldrums. It was just part of the deal and something for which everyone aboard prepared. And they were not alone. Sea lanes around the Horn became busy, to the extent that there was nearly always a good possibility another vessel would be spotted. It might be sailing the same direction or the opposite, and it might even need assistance. Such traffic meant there was a risk of collision, which became another major concern. These shipping lanes became the maritime highway for the world during the second half of the nineteenth century, and they represented the true glory days of sailing around Cape Horn.[68]

In 1850, Damariscotta's Metcalf & Norris Shipyard was one of the first to build a clipper, the 764-ton *Alert*. It went right into the California trade.

Launched in November 1850 with Francis Bursley as its master, it departed New York and arrived in San Francisco after 150 days. Its 1853 voyage from New York to San Francisco took 148 days, the weather off Cape Horn again delaying them for more than two weeks. In 1858, the *Alert* was lost with several officers and half of its crew off the coast of Formosa, today's Taiwan, in the China Sea. The 610-ton clipper ship *Grey Feather* was built by C.S. Huston in Eastport in 1850. It made the 1851 California run under Daniel McLaughlin in 138 days (another source says 136), only to see upon its arrival the smoldering ruins of San Francisco due to the great fire of May 3, 1851. The ship later made a better record in 1852 with a run of 126 days; it was one of the most remarkable Cape Horn races of all time, a contest that involved fifteen different clipper ships. By 1855, the *Grey Feather* was engaged in the Australian trade, although it made an 1858 New York–San Francisco run in 128 days. It was eventually sold at Bremen in 1862, renamed *Ida*.[69]

In 1855, the Bath-built Maine clipper *Monsoon* took thirty days to double Cape Horn. At one point, they lost all their anchors but made use of a cannon in its place, finally arriving after 157 days. The 158-foot long 773-ton clipper had been built in 1851 for Trufant & Drummond. Its 1852 run took 130 days, and in 1854, it was the first ship to arrive that calendar year on January 4, having taken 120 days. The Rockland-built 1852 clipper *Defiance* made its initial California run in 160 days, after being sent to Rio de Janeiro for repairs. They reported head winds most of the way and very heavy weather off of Cape Horn. When it was launched in December 1852, the Frankfort-built 944-ton clipper ship *Flying Arrow* had no figurehead. Originally intended to be *Flying Yankee*, a quick sale to new owners renamed it, and a billet replaced the figurehead position. The name change and missing figurehead were the first of many challenges and disasters. *Flying Arrow* had a difficult maiden voyage and faced severe weather off of Cape Horn on its return voyage to New York. Its main topgallant mast was carried away and its topmast was sprung in very heavy gales, but *Flying Arrow* completed its run in 143 days.[70]

One of the more durable 1852 Maine-built clippers was *Flying Eagle*. It made a dozen California runs and Cape Horn passages and suffered partial dismastings on over half of them. Its maiden California run was completed in 167 days, including time in Rio de Janeiro after it lost its main topmast and all gear attached only 5 days out. The 1854 California run was just as troublesome, taking *Flying Eagle* 134 days, including 10 days off of Cape Horn with no foretopgallant mast and main yard. Both had been carried away by storms. It made the 1855 run in 124 days, again

facing a tough Horn passage, this time with 15 days of heavy gales and lost or split sails. The 1856 run was made in 118 days, and this time, it was a lost jib-boom and bowsprit cap. The 1858 run was completed in 132 days, taking 21 days off Cape Horn facing severe gales. The 1859 run was done in 153 days, including time for a lost bowsprit off the Horn. The 1860 run took 160 days, and they doubled the Horn in 18 days. During the 1862 run, *Flying Eagle* faced 24 continuous days of heavy gales off Cape Horn. Its 1863 Horn passage went smoothly, but the next two runs each encountered more than three-week periods before they could double it.[71]

The 514-ton Robbinston clipper *Juniper* was built in 1852 and made the 1853 California run in 208 days, most notably due to spending 49 days to double Cape Horn.[72] The *Golden Racer*, originally launched as *Hyperion*, made the 1853 run in 130 days, facing 19 days of continuous bad weather off the Horn. The *Golden Racer*'s main topmast was sprung, and its spars were damaged. In the 1854 run, which was accomplished in 151 days, the clipper ship lost its main yard while off of Cape Horn.[73]

In 1853, Maine reached its peak with clipper ship construction. The Rockland-built *Anglo Saxon* was described as handsome, but it never made any fast passages around Cape Horn. Its maiden California run took 150 days, mostly due to horrendous South Atlantic weather in which the clipper lost its deck load. The *Anglo Saxon* then faced bad weather for another 26 days off the Horn, where it lost its jib-boom. The 1858 run took a dreadful 164 days due to very light winds most of the way and then constant southwest gales off the cape, which took over 40 days to double. The 1859 California run was completed in 142 days, 26 of which were spent battling weather off of Cape Horn. The 1860 run took 137 days, 18 of which were spent doubling the Horn. The *Anglo Saxon*'s last passage in 1862 took 41 days to double. During the Civil War, the clipper was captured and burned off Kinsale, England, by the Confederate cruiser *Florida*.[74]

The 1853-built heavily sparred clipper *Black Warrior* boasted three complete decks for cargo. Built in Newcastle or Damariscotta, it made the 1855 California run in 124 days, 36 of which were spent in heavy gales off Cape Stiff. There, the *Black Warrior* lost its foretopsail yard and split its sails.[75] Another 1853 Damariscotta-built clipper, the *Wild Rover*, made its 1856 California run in 127 days in light weather, except for 26 days of extreme storms off of the Horn. Under Searsport captain J.C. Nichols, the *Wild Rover* made a great run from New York to San Francisco in 107 days. But its 1859 run took 173 days, including two full months clawing its away around the Horn. On four separate occasions during

that voyage, the *Wild Rover* passed the rocky cape, only to be driven back by fierce winds. In 1868, on its last Cape Horn passage, the *Wild Rover* took three weeks to double. The clipper eventually went aground at Jones Inlet on Long Island in 1871.[76]

Another 1853-built clipper ship, the *Flying Dragon*, made five western Cape Horn passages between 1850 and 1860. Built in Bath by Trufant & Drummond, its figurehead was an open-mouthed dragon head with a protruding tongue. It was fastest of the Maine-built California clippers, and it was the only one from the state to make the run in less than 100 days. But it also completed the 1853 California run in 148 days, 35 of which were spent off of Cape Horn, where they lost the jib-boom and sprung their bowsprit and foreyard. Captain Judah P. Baker of Brewster also passed away that voyage. A 1,400-ton extreme clipper of the same name was launched the same year at Winterport, but records suggest this clipper must have been lost soon after.[77]

Other 1853 Maine-built clippers included the *Viking*, *Gauntlet* and *Wild Wave*. The *Viking* sported a Scandinavian warrior in armor as a figurehead. Described as a half-clipper and built by Trufant & Drummond in Bath, the *Viking* was 230 feet long, 41 feet in beam and drew 21 feet. It made six respectable California runs. The longest was its 1859 run, which it made in 133 days, as it spent two weeks off Cape Horn, and 3 of those days saw the clipper completely hedged in by ice. Winds drove it back, and they were forced to make a second attempt. In June 1863, the *Viking* was en route from Hong Kong to San Francisco, carrying 500 people, when it ran aground on the rocks of Onegahama Beach on Mikurashima, a small island 140 miles south of Tokyo. According to a commemorative plaque, through the intervention of local authorities and islander hospitality, 23 crew members and 460 Chinese passengers were saved.[78]

The Richmond-built *Gauntlet* was the largest Maine clipper of the day, and it was the sharpest built north of Portsmouth. Thomas J. Southard built the 240-foot clipper for Stephenson & Thurston. Its 1854 run from New York to Callao took 94 days, with 18 of them being spent rounding the Horn in horrendous weather. Its 1858 California run took 161 days. The *Gauntlet* was sold to the British in 1860, renamed *Sunda* and burned in 1878. Another Richmond-built clipper, the *Wild Wave*, made its 1857 California run in 140 days, 20 of which were spent in heavy Cape Horn weather. Off the Horn, its main topgallant mast was carried away, and its mainsails split.[79]

The 1,520-ton 1853-built clipper *Spitfire* sported a gilded eagle figurehead. Built by Frankfort resident John Arey, it was considered the

most beautiful and fastest of the clippers. The *Spitfire* made its 1853 California run in under 100 days after facing storms for 15 days off the Horn. They were 380 miles from San Francisco and only 87 days out. The *Spitfire* set an 1854 record after taking only 65 days to sail from Rio de Janeiro to San Francisco, making the complete California run in 119 days, even with a severe Cape Horn gale. On its 1860 voyage, the *Spitfire* found itself in a race with the *Black Hawk*. The *Spitfire* had departed from Boston on December 21, the same day the *Black Hawk* passed Sandy Hook. Both arrived in San Francisco on April 8—both took 107 days. Its 1862 run was completed in 127 days, 22 of which were spent doubling the Horn. The *Spitfire* was eventually sold to the British and was still in service in 1869.[80]

The 1853 Robbinston-built clipper *Red Gauntlet*'s 1855 run took 194 days, after being sent to Valparaiso for repairs. It had taken nearly a month to round the Horn; its rudder-head was broken, its cutwater and stem started, an entire set of sails and some spars were lost and it had five feet of water in its hold. All hands, including Captain Thomas Andrew's wife, suffered dreadfully from the cold, wet conditions. His wife, whose name was not recorded, barely slept during their twenty-nine days off of Cape Horn, but she helped nurse injured sailors and kept brewed tea available for crew. In 1861, the *Red Gauntlet* made another New York–San Francisco run, taking 148 days to complete, again delayed by horrible weather off Cape Horn. On one voyage, the *Red Gauntlet* faced a hurricane that lasted fifty-six hours. The log records:

> [The ship was] *struck by a sea which carried away the fore channels and drew bolts of top gallant backstays out of sides, losing fore and main top gallant masts, and starting upper works forward. At 1 AM, shipped a sea which went through the main spencer, taking larboard quarter and stern boats, staving bulwarks midship houses and taking everything moveable about decks with water. At 4 AM, blew away a new main topsail from the close reef.*[81]

In 1863, the clipper ship was captured by the Confederate raider *Florida*. Before it was set on fire, five *Red Gauntlet* crewmen volunteered to serve on the enemy ship.[82]

The 1854-built *Crest of the Wave*'s life was mostly unfortunate. Built in Warren, the 942-ton clipper made its 1858 California run in 163 days, 36 of which were spent in bad weather off of Cape Horn. In November 1862,

during a run from New York to Valparaiso, it endured a lengthy stay at Port Stanley in the Falklands due to a lost rudder and other damage. The 1864 voyage to Valparaiso was even worse. Many crew members, including the captain's wife and first mate, died of yellow fever. The remaining men, sick and ineffective, left the captain practically alone to handle the ship. Around April 14, 1870, while on a voyage from Liverpool to Baltimore, during a severe gale, the *Crest of the Wave* struck Wreck Island, fifteen miles north of Cape Charles, and it was lost with all twenty hands. After the wreck, two of the ship's boats washed ashore. One contained three bodies and the other the body of its captain. The clipper's flag and a portion of its quarter-board were later recovered.[83]

The 1854 clipper *Euterpe*'s captain was John Arey of Frankfort, the town where it had been built. The *Euterpe* raced the fellow Maine-built *Talisman* around the Cape Horn in 1858; both ships made the run in 135 days. The *Euterpe* took 19 days to double the Horn, its hatch-house and quarter boat stove in and sails split. Sold in 1867, in 1871, it was abandoned off of Brazil with a major leak while running from Peru, around Cape Horn, to Falmouth, England. The mate and eight crew members were lost. The 1854 Bath-built clipper *Mary Robinson*'s six San Francisco runs earned it a reputation for its timely delivery of cargo in first-class condition. Built by Trufant & Drummond,

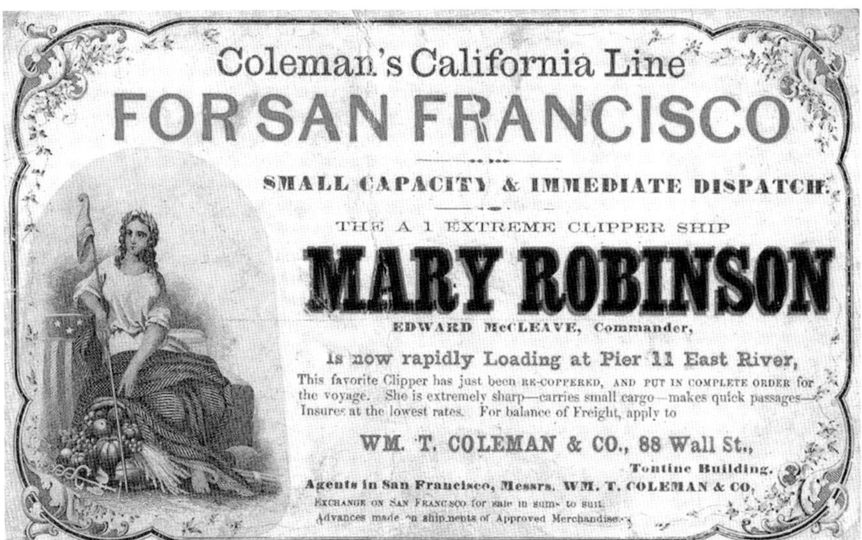

The clipper ship *Mary Robinson*'s sailing card, nineteenth century. *Courtesy of the Library of Congress.*

the *Mary Robinson* made its 1854 California run in 134 days, which included a month spent off the Horn in gales and heavy snowstorms and 4 days at Valparaiso for repairs. The 1854 Damariscotta-built clipper *Talisman* made five passages to San Francisco. Its 1859 run took 142 days, including the two months it spent battling atrocious Cape Horn weather. In 1863, it sailed from New York to Shanghai but ran afoul of the Confederate raider *Alabama*, which took possession of the ship and stripped it of cargo and weaponry, including four brass twelve-pound cannons. The *Talisman* was then burned. The 1855 Rockland-built clipper *Young Mechanic* made the 1862 California run in 127 days, with 25 of those days spent doubling the Horn, where its main yard was lost. It later burned at sea in 1866.[84]

Rockland native Captain Joshua Patten of extreme clipper *Neptune's Car* made the Horn passage twice with his twenty-year old wife, Mary, at his side. While he managed the ship, Mary worked with new wind charts that had recently been produced by Matthew F. Maury. It was hoped that these charts would help Cape Horn vessels shave weeks off their passages. On their 1855 passage, Patten fell ill as they approached the Horn. The troublesome first mate at the time sat in irons, and an inexperienced twenty-year-old second left no one in charge. Patten's wife, Mary, pregnant with their first child, ended up navigating the ship safely around the dangerous cape, all the way to San Francisco. According to the *New York Daily Tribune*:

> *About one week after the captain fell sick, the mate wrote a letter to Mrs. Patten, reminding her of the dangers of the coast and the great responsibility she had assumed, and offering to take charge of the ship. She replied that, in the judgment of her husband, he was unfit to be mate, and therefore could not be considered qualified to fill the post of commander. Stung by this rebuff, the fellow tried to stir up the crew to mutiny against her; but she called the other mates and sailors aft and appealed to them to support her in her hour of trial. To a man, they resolved to stand by her and the ship, come what might. It was pleasant to witness their cheerful obedience to her orders, as each man vied with his fellows in the performance of his duties.*

For eighteen days, they battled heavy westerly storms before *Neptune's Car* doubled the Horn. It was reported that when it reached port, vessel and cargo arrived in better trim than any competitor.[85]

The 1852 Maine-built 1,336-ton clipper *Queen of the Pacific*'s short life was filled with mishaps. Built in Pembroke, its 1853 California run took 193 days. The clipper took 30 days to double Cape Horn, it lost its topmast and

developed a severe leak. The clipper was sent to Valparaiso, where it found that a portion of its ice cargo had melted, which affected ship's performance. Condemned in 1857 after being dismasted in an Atlantic hurricane, it was repaired to make the 1858 California run in 131 days on short rations. When its iron water tank was ruptured by shifting cargo, the crew were allowed only one pint of fresh water daily. Its 1859 run from New York to San Francisco ended in disaster. The *Queen of the Pacific* foundered on a reef 180 miles north of Pernambuco. Part of its guano cargo was saved, but the clipper broke in two amidships and was a total loss.[86]

The medium 1,194-ton clipper *King Philip* was built in Alna. It was launched in 1856 with a wooden hull and three masts. It was named for Metacomet, the Wampanoag war chief known as King Philip. Seven years later, the *King Philip* was advertised as "a strictly first-class clipper ship with quick dispatch" and "well-known to shippers as one of the best and most reliable vessels in the California trade." It carried cargo to San Francisco and called at Baker Island for guano. This route included Cape Horn passages, and two involved mutinies. The *King Philip* was even set on fire both times. In 1878, it wrecked when a San Francisco tugboat dropped its tow, causing the clipper to drift toward Ocean Beach, just outside the city. It ran aground in heavy surf and broke apart. Considered

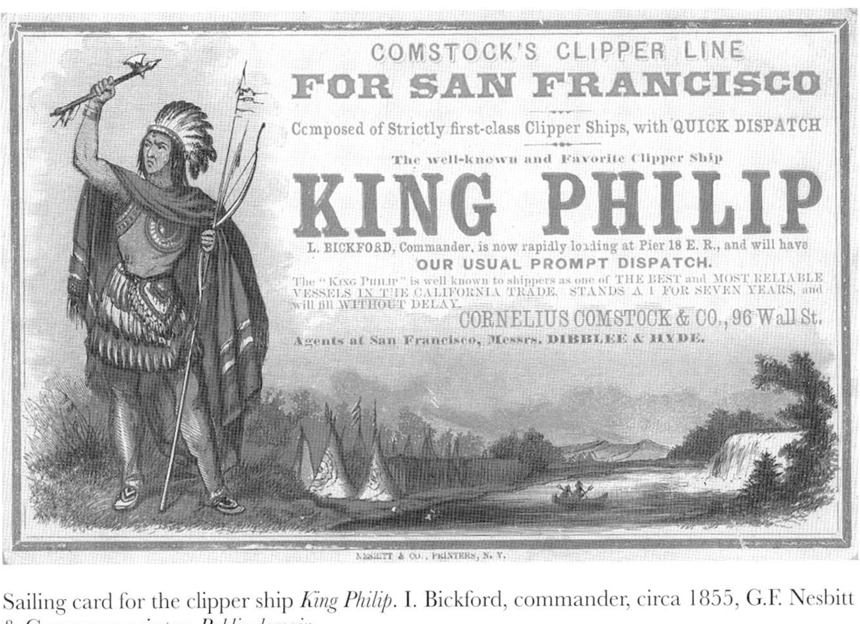

Sailing card for the clipper ship *King Philip*. I. Bickford, commander, circa 1855, G.F. Nesbitt & Company, printer. *Public domain.*

to be the "most complete remains of an American medium clipper," remnants reappear every so often from the sands.[87]

The age of Maine-built clippers was brief, overcome by high maintenance, rising costs for large crews and a low carrying capacity. Even before the Civil War ended, clippers were on the wane, but the need for transport continued. Maine met this new challenge by developing the down-easters, adding them to its merchant fleet. These ships were modifications of the clipper; they had a similar bow but had a larger cargo capacity and better handling. These larger vessels mastered the balance between speed and tonnage. They also required one-third of the crew used on clippers. From the 1860s until the 1930s, square-rigged down-easters delivered cargoes, such as grain and kerosene, around the world. They proved quite adept in Cape Horn waters.[88]

Early forerunners proved their sturdiness for Cape Horn travel. The 1854 449-ton bark *Lizzie Boggs* was launched in Warren. In 1861, Rockland newspapers stated the *Lizzie Boggs* owners' intentions of running it from Bordeaux, France, to San Francisco by way of Cape Horn. When it arrived in California that September, stories were told of dreadful weather off the Horn. While hove to and just barely underway, with only a foretopmast staysail, the *Lizzie Boggs* shipped a sea that stove its monkey rails, started its waterways and head and caused a leak in the upper-works. Repairs had still not been completed before its arrival in San Francisco. The 277-ton East Machias bark *Olive Jane* was built in 1862 and sailed from Cutler to Boston and then on to Valparaiso, barely surviving its first Cape Horn doubling. Rockland's *Martha Cobb*, built same year as *Olive Jane*, made its initial Horn passage as a chartered ship carrying general cargo for San Francisco. Lacking clipper speed, especially in Cape Horn waters, Captain Thomas R. Pillsbury referred to the *Martha Cobb* as the "wharf."[89]

On its maiden New York–San Francisco voyage, Sewall's Bath-built down-easter *Carrollton* faced forty-one days of gales while doubling Cape Horn. It survived only to nearly be capsized in May 1877 by a tidal wave at the Peruvian guano fields, the result of a huge earthquake. That tidal wave struck the Tarapaca Coast, destroying nitrate and guano ports and fleets; at least thirteen vessels were lost, including the 1862 Belfast-built bark *Shamrock* at Punta de Lobos, Northern Chile. For years, it had engaged in the Cape Horn guano run.[90]

The Sewall down-easter *Occidental* sailed from San Francisco to Ireland and experienced such heavy gales off of Cape Horn that the practice of heavily loading these ships and sending them in that direction was

Painting of the ship *Eliza McNeil* of Thomaston off Cape Horn. *Courtesy of the Thomaston Historical Society.*

questioned. Captain Joe Sewall wrote the owners complaining of lack of seaworthiness in such heavily loaded vessels in such bad weather. Bath native Captain Frederic S. Bosworth took Sewall-built ship *Harvester* to San Francisco in 1880 and faced a full month of tremendously heavy westerly gales off Cape Horn. He later wrote that it was the most prolonged and difficult experience of his entire maritime career.[91]

In 1877, the 1,449-ton Waldoboro-built down-easter *Willie Reed*, considered the best ship built there, was launched. It is credited with a quick eastward passage from San Francisco to Dublin in 114 days. Twice while rounding Cape Horn to the west, the *Willie Reed* outperformed the nearby Thomaston-built ship *Eliza McNeil*. *Willie Reed*'s last westward Horn passage took 153 days to reach Astoria, Oregon, from New York. In 1894, it wrecked at Point San Quentin in Royan, France, a total loss. The *Eliza McNeil*, eventually sold at Antwerp, is pictured off of Cape Horn in George Wharton Rice's 1938 publication *The Shipping Days of Old Boothbay from the Revolution to the World War*.[92]

Captain John Brown Emerson's account *Round the Horn by Captain John* was taken from his logbook and is housed at the Penobscot Marine Museum. On February 27, they crossed 50 degrees south latitude at

Eliza McNeil at Thomaston, 1871. *Courtesy of the Thomaston Historical Society.*

midnight, then passed through the Straits of LeMaire with two other vessels, one from Waldoboro, in weather "as mild as summer at home." On March 7, they had a fine view of the cape, but then it began to blow. A strong current did not help their progress, and they found it "hard to make southwesterly for three days in that locality." They doubled the Horn on February 24 in twenty-five days.[93]

During the 1870s, Thomaston almost exclusively supplied tonnage for the San Francisco line of ships. For that decade and the next, its Cape Horn down-easters sailed with general cargo to California or with case oil (kerosene) to Japan. Both routes involved doubling the Horn. The bark *Frank Curling* was going out of Cardiff, headed to San Francisco with a cargo of coal, when it sank off of Cape Horn during a hurricane. Its captain, the namesake of the ship, tried to go too fast. When its coal cargo shifted in the storm, the *Frank Curling* turned turtle, and half the crew was lost; Frank Curling survived. He headed for Cape Horn once more on the *Joseph Spinney*. In deep southern waters, they saved eight native islanders in an open canoe. For eight days, seven men and a boy had been blown 260 miles from land. When Curling sighted them, they were emaciated, and one had died. The others decided to kill the sixteen-

year-old to nourish themselves and were preparing to do so when the *Joseph Spinney* came into view.[94]

Built in Waldoboro—at the time, its largest vessel—the 1,660-ton *Emily Reed* was launched in 1880. In 1885, the 209-foot square-rigged down-easter had its cargo shifted while off of Cape Horn. Its spars were sprung, and most of its fresh water was lost; it was an ordeal they barely survived. Three years later, after another tough Horn passage, the *Emily Reed* was sent to Valparaiso for repairs and to restore its cargo, which had also shifted. During an eastbound rounding in 1890, the *Emily Reed* faced heavy gales. For nearly four days, the ship wallowed in heavy seas, more submerged than afloat. Its forecastle was stove in, and eight sailors were lost overboard. The following year, the *Emily Reed* encountered more bad weather off Cape Horn; this time, its rudder-head was sprung. They were forced back, limping into Rio de Janeiro for a new rudder. Captain O.D. Sheldon resigned his command, thinking himself the cause of such bad luck. The *Emily Reed* spent its career on the West Coast and was lost on February 14, 1908, when it went ashore near Nehelem Bay.[95]

In November 1888, the Bath Sewall Company sent its schooner *Carrie A. Lane* around Cape Horn to San Francisco. The following January, it sent its new four-mast schooner the *Douglas Dearborn* eastward, past the Cape of Good Hope to Sydney, Australia, then around Cape Horn on its return voyage. It was the *Douglas Dearborn*'s only Horn voyage. These experiments were to test the vessels' efficacy, handling and capability for withstanding grueling voyages. North Haven native Captain Fred Dyer wrote that the *Carrie A. Lane* experienced extreme difficulty when doubling Cape Horn, taking forty-seven days to do so. They met a series of westerly gales, which blew out their sails, flooded the cabin and nearly caused a mutiny:

> *It is a mistake to think that this rig on a schooner as large as the* Carrie A. Lane *and heavy rigged can make good time around Cape Horn. The sea there…when it falls calm as it did many times with me, the wear and tear to sails and rigging is something dreadful. My peak halyards are all broke down. Will have to have new sheaves, most of the running rigging will have to be new.*[96]

When the four-mast Bath bark *Shenandoah* was built by Arthur Sewall and launched on Thanksgiving 1890, it was the largest wooden sailing vessel in the world, their second in a fleet of four. At 3,407 tons, the *Shenandoah* seemed destined to revive the Cape Horn trade. Thus, it was with much

sadness that Captain James P. Murphy wrote to the owners, describing how he had needed to put the crew to work on pumps thirty minutes for every hour from Cape Horn to Liverpool. He noted that the *Shenandoah* leaked five inches an hour while at sea.

> *This ship from her poop forward works and bends both sideways and up and down and, to my mind, is getting worse every passage. Have seen her bow lift 3 ft and then fall back.…Then in running in heavy seas, have seen her bow go sideways. When sighting the masts in line, the foremast head go*[es] *out of line and back from head of mainmast 4 feet.*[97]

Murphy also reported that they lost a fine sailor, who had been washed overboard while off Cape Horn.[98]

On its 1892 voyage to San Francisco, the *Shenandoah* met up with the British ship *Old Kensington* off of Cape Horn. To their dismay, the *Shenandoah*'s crew watched as *Old Kensington* gained on them, and "as she passed…her crew manned the rigging and derisively cheered." Three days later in a furious gale with bulwarks smashed, it was *Old Kensington*'s turn to watch as *Shenandoah* "went foaming by her close-hauled under a press of canvas clawing out to windward in magnificent fashion and behaving splendidly in the face of the Cape Stiff greybeards." The *Shenandoah* reached San Francisco in 111 days; *Old Kensington* had to retreat in distress to Port Stanley in the Falklands to repair extensive damage suffered off the Horn. They finally reached San Francisco after 348 days.[99]

Newcastle native Captain Omar Chapman sailed the *Shenandoah* in April 1905 around Cape Horn without mishap, only to encounter a fierce hurricane on the Pacific side.

> [I had to run] *before the wind and sea for two days, as she labored and strained so badly…her bow would rise and fall four or five feet and work from side to side as much or more…we could just keep her free by steam.… Since then, we have been pumping constantly by hand with ten minutes rest every hour and can just keep her free with one pump.…I can carry very little sail, as any pressure makes her leak so badly that we cannot handle it. We have pumped her constantly for 22 days, 3,250 miles. My crew are getting tired out. The pumps are getting worn badly.*[100]

Chapman went to Valparaiso for repairs and caulking. The *Shenandoah* remained on the Cape Horn run until 1910, when it was finally sold. Captain

James P. Murphy had commanded the *Shenandoah* on its first and last voyages. Finally, while it was being used as a barge, it collided with the steamer *Powhatan* and sank off of Fire Island, New York, on October 29, 1915.[101]

The Sewall-built *Susquehanna* arrived San Francisco in November 1895, reporting extreme weather off of Cape Horn. The captain said the main deck had worked considerably, and every main deck scupper on the waterway seam had broken. He noted in several places that one could see the main deck planks move back and forth in bad seas. In 1898, the *Susquehanna* experienced a severe winter doubling of Cape Horn, taking them over two weeks. One sailor wrote:

> *Two men were at the wheel, all gear, ratlines, halyards, etc. were coated with ice, waves were dashing over the ship. There were ropes stretched over the decks to hang on to so we would not be swept overboard. While we all had oilskins on, these were only good to keep the wind out, as we were all wet through.*[102]

Upon entering calmer waters, the *Susquehanna*'s crew had to use knives to cut off their salt-encrusted clothing, including their underwear.[103] In June 1896, another Sewall-built ship, the *William Rosenfield*, made a great voyage with a load of nitrates from Caleta Buena in northern Chile to New York. Upon its arrival, the captain reported that, even with their swift passage, they had been held up for days off of Cape Horn by more icebergs than could be counted. The down-easter had made its maiden Cape Horn passage in late 1885 from Baltimore to San Francisco with a load of coal. Gardiner native Captain William Dunphy wrote they had had no bad weather until they were off the Horn. He noted:

> [The ship then acted] *terrible bad….With a strong wind, I could not carry but little canvas. She would ship heavy seas and flood the main deck…she disabled several of the men….I think that if I had encountered a sever gale, she would have washed bulwarks, houses away. Perhaps gone down. She would settle down like a block of marble….A vessel could not behave worse.*[104]

In 1903, the Sewall-built *Edward Sewall* was off of Cape Horn when its side-port beam sprung. Before they could fix it, seven feet of water filled the ship's hold. It took them two weeks of continuous pumping to clear it.[105] In 1908, the ship was again in Horn waters when the link to its fore

yard truss broke, which brought a ninety-six-foot-tall steel spar crashing down, landing half overboard, with the big sail dragging in the water. This made them roll heavily enough to founder. Taking four days to clear the mess and rebuild the truss, they used the ship's stove as a forge. It took another eight days before calmer weather enabled them to cross the yard again. In 1909, the *Edward Sewall* was again off of Cape Horn, this time, in winter. Its second mate washed overboard, and its first mate was badly injured. He was laid up for nearly a month before he went insane. Another sailor on this voyage also broke down. Fifteen of the *Edward Sewall*'s sails were blown to pieces. In 1913, the down-easter sailed from Philadelphia to Seattle and took sixty-seven days to double Cape Horn. Three times they passed the cape, but each time they were blown back. On one try, they got three hundred miles beyond the cape but were then blown backward until they were forty miles east of the Horn. Bath resident Captain Richard Quick lost two fingers during this epic battle with Cape Horn.[106]

In 1907, the Sewall-owned ship *Kenilworth* sailed for California but spent two months battling its way around Cape Horn. It failed and finally went to Montevideo in distress with its sails shredded, steering gear broken and spars in need of repair. The *Kenilworth* set out in April but failed again to round the cape. Instead, it sailed east for the Cape of Good Hope, but it failed to round that cape either. Demoralized, it reached Rio de Janeiro in September 1907 and was given a new captain. It eventually made its way to San Francisco and was then sold to the Alaska Packers Association and renamed *Star of Scotland*. It was later torpedoed by a German submarine off the coast of Southwest Africa, near the Cape of Good Hope.[107]

Albert Nickels Blanchard was perhaps the most famous of Searsport's captains. In 1905, from Philadelphia to Honolulu, he was captain of the *Bangalore*. In Cape Horn waters, Blanchard discovered that his cargo was on fire, but they were able to make it to Valparaiso. On another Horn voyage, Blanchard captained the *Herbert Black*. Just before reaching Cape Horn waters, it lost its rudder.

> [Captain Blanchard] *succeeded in building a jury rudder, rounded the cape, and reached his destination. After calling at a number of different ports on the coast, he returned around Cape Horn to New York under the jury rudder—a feat which is believed never to have been equaled. The scars made by the chains controlling the improvised rudder were visible in the planking under the runs for many years.*[108]

In 1912, Chapman sailed Sewall's *Dirigo* on its California run, deciding to take the more dangerous shortcut through Strait of LeMaire. Its passengers included the famous novelist Jack London and his wife. The *Dirigo* nearly wrecked on the remote Wollaston Island. Jack London went on to fashion his story *The Mutiny of the Elsinore* on their experience.[109]

Many Maine captains, sailors and Maine-built ships set records in their battles off of Cape Horn. The town of Searsport produced many notable ship captains who doubled the Horn in respectable time. Frank L. Carver sailed the *Erskine M. Phelps* from Iquiqui on the Pacific coast of Latin America to New York in 84 days. Daniel Smith Goodell rounded the Horn twice in the *Brown Brothers* when sailing from San Francisco to Havre and back in 8 months and 12 days. Phineas Pendleton captained the *Henry B. Hyde* from San Francisco to Liverpool in 95 days. The clipper ship *Warner* made the 1852 California run in 140 days via Valparaiso and then had a great return trip from San Francisco to New York the same year that, at the time, was thought to be a record. It never seemed to get the clipper ship the recognition it deserved. One source states that the *Warner*'s performances possessed "clipperly qualities in a high degree." The *Warner* was reported missing, along with all hands, including Captain Luther Ripley Jr., in March 1854.[110]

There is an 1851 oil painting of the *Warren* rounding Cape Horn by artist James Edward Buttersworth. The ship was built in 1851 at South Portland by Alford Butler in the same yard as the clipper *Snow Squall*. The painting was made to document the chance close encounter of the two ships in bad seas off of Cape Horn. The crew on watch aboard each vessel can be seen grouped forward of the foremast. This was a common place of shelter for the watch. The painting was gifted by Elizabeth B. Noyce to Bath's Maine Maritime Museum.[111]

James Arey & Sons of Frankfort built the *Spitfire* in 1853. On its maiden voyage from Boston to San Francisco, the ship neared Cape Horn in bad weather. The *Spitfire* badly sprung its topmasts and bowsprit and went to Rio de Janeiro for repairs. It still managed to arrive in San Francisco in under one hundred days. Another local Searsport resident and immigrant from Denmark, Captain James Frank Peterson, got his maritime start when he sailed with his uncle to France for a cargo of wine and liquors, which they then took around Cape Horn to San Francisco.[112]

The 536-ton bark *Comet* was considered the fastest and most successful Maine clipper ship ever built. Launched in Pembroke in 1852, it had large elegantly furnished cabins, a toilet, smoking rooms, bathrooms and a fine

library. The *Comet*'s first New York–San Francisco run took 103 days. It made the 1852 California run in 126 days and the 1853 run in 133 days, both through horrible conditions off of Cape Horn. On one return run, the *Comet* raced the *Flying Dutchman* back to New York, oftentimes within pistol-shot distances of each other. The Maine clipper arrived one day earlier than its rival. The *Comet* made a run to New York in 1854 in 76 days and 7 hours, a record from San Francisco to any North American port that remains to this day. Its Cape Horn doubling time has never been beaten. The *Comet* went on to the London–China trade and then made more California runs. It was sold, renamed *Fiery Star* and put into the Australian trade. It caught fire on a later voyage and was abandoned, with most of its crew and passengers filling the boats. Seventeen others, including the captain, elected to stay on board. In an ironic twist, the boats were never heard from again, but the nineteen who gave up their seats were later saved by a passing ship. The clipper was salvaged, renamed *Hokulele* and listed as still sailing in 1891.[113]

The 1852 clipper *Rattler* was described as being razor sharp and was known as "Deacon's clipper" due to its owner, Deacon George Thomas. The *Rattler* doubled Cape Horn going west four times between 1850 and 1860—eight total in its career. The 1852 California run took 121 days, the 1853 run was made in 121 days, the 1858 run took 115 days and the 1859 run took 160 days. The *Rattler*'s best, in 1853, would have been better save for the three weeks of heavy gales off Cape Horn. In 1858, the *Rattler* took just 7 days to double the Horn but faced delays elsewhere. It also served as troop transport to Crimea and as a regular Havre packet ship. By 1878, as the Costa Rican ship *Martha*, the clipper still posted a record run from Callao to San Francisco of just 28 days. In 1890, after thirty-eight years of hard service, the ship was broken up for junk for $2,300.[114]

Robbinston's *Moses Taylor* was a 997-ton ship built in 1852. It doubled Cape Horn numerous times in its first six years. Another Robbinston-built vessel, the *Charles P. Moore* (or *Moure*), was a 330-ton bark built in 1855. It, too, was put into the California trade. After many stormy Cape Horn crossings, the *Charles P. Moore* was renamed the *Betsena*, then later, *Tabor*, and in 1864, it made its homeport in Valparaiso.[115]

In 1888, Waldoboro launched the first five-mast Atlantic schooner, the *Governor Ames*, from Leverett Storer's shipyard. In 1890, a Baltimore–San Francisco run took 143 days. The *Governor Ames* was the only five-mast ship to successfully weather Cape Horn on a westward passage, although its captain was adamant about not repeating the adventure. Many Horn vessels received little notice. In eight years, from 1890 to 1898, the Thomaston-built *Edward*

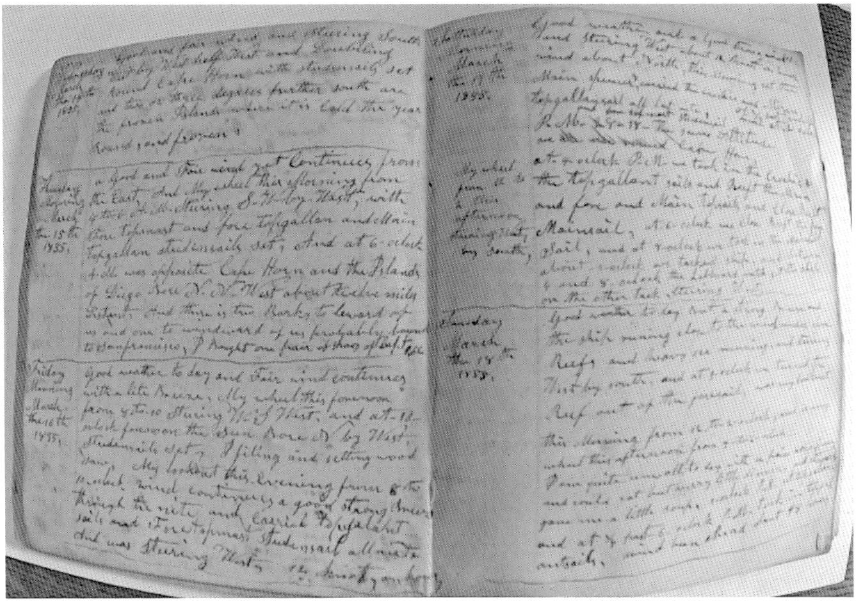

Journal of P.B.F. Bassatt aboard brig *Francisco* around Cape Horn. *Photograph by Charles H. Lagerbom, from the Penobscot Marine Museum.*

O'Brien rounded Cape Horn nine times and the Cape of Good Hope twice. It just did its job, according to one source, "like people of the same type who accomplish much, though they never make the headlines."[116]

Although it was not built in Maine, but Amesbury, Massachusetts, the *Polly* had both Maine and Cape Horn connections. The forty-eight-ton schooner, launched in 1806, was sixty-one feet long and twenty feet in beam, drawing a fathom of water. Between launch and 1910, *Polly* had multiple owners. For years, it worked in Penobscot Bay, as its then owner was from Prospect. Starting in 1849, the *Polly* doubled Cape Horn six times, twice when circumnavigating the world. On April 26, 1874, at Owls Head, it went ashore in a gale and was still on the beach when it was purchased by Captain Lewis A. Arey, who used the *Polly* until 1885. At the end of its life, one of the *Polly*'s original anchors still hung from its cathead. It was broken up for firewood in 1918 in Quincy, Massachusetts.[117]

One Cape Horn journal in the Penobscot Marine Museum collection is from P.B.F. Bassatt, and he kept it in 1855 aboard the brig *Francisco*. In March, they approached Cape Horn in good weather, which continued until the strong breeze became stronger. On March 20, Bassatt recorded, "Had quite rough weather through the past nite [*sic*] and heavy squalls

of wind, all hands called in the nite [*sic*] and in the forenoon to reef the sails and very heavy sea running, and a brig a little to windward of us and ship lays her course north by west."[118]

In 1867, Joseph Clark of Waldoboro built 1,258-ton full-rigged ship *Gold Hunter*. It proved a profitable vessel in its thirteen-year career in the Cape Horn trade; Waldoboro residents owned ⅝ of the vessel. One voyage involved a collision with another ship on entering the San Francisco Bay. The *Gold Hunter*'s most difficult Horn trip occurred when, in turbulent seas, its rudder head and the top of the main vertical timber of the rudder known as the main piece were twisted off. The *Gold Hunter* continued to San Francisco under tackles. The down-easter was eventually lost on a reef in the South China Sea, a total loss.[119]

Searsport native and ship captain Jeremiah Grant Park was born on December 9, 1849. He was master of the *Acme* from 1910 to 1914. In 1911, the *Acme* carried 2.9 million feet of lumber, the largest cargo ever carried around Cape Horn in a sailing vessel. He died in November 1916, lost at sea off Ireland's west coast, when his ship the *Magna Reva* reported by wireless that it was in distress. The report added that the boats were gone and that the vessel was drifting before the wind. The message was heard, and the area was searched by SS *Rockingham*, but neither the *Magna Reva* nor Park was ever found.[120]

The Carter family members of Woolwich were also renowned deep-water sailors. Captain Edward L. Carter's papers, including those from his thirty-six-years as captain, are housed at the Maine Maritime Museum in Bath. He and brother Christopher Otis Carter engaged in the San Francisco trade, with many doublings of Cape Horn as well as the Cape of Good Hope. As down-easter captains, the Carters often took their families with them. From Woolwich, the brothers' retired shipmaster father, Captain Charles William Carter, shared news about the family and the town and reported on business conditions, family concerns and Bath ship arrivals and departures. They, in turn, wrote of their travels, including Cape Horn conditions and rates of progress around it. On his last Cape Horn rounding in 1891, Edward L. Carter died while aboard the *Parthia* in San Francisco, after the ship's maiden voyage.[121]

Searsport native Captain Clifton Curtis was born on June 4, 1858. In February 1888, while serving as first officer of the Pennsylvania-built steel ship *Tillie E. Starbuck*, Curtis entered the forecastle to stop a riot. He broke up the fight but was stabbed by one of the mutineers. After being taken to a hospital, he took a long time to heal. A thank-you card that was sent to him was printed in October 1891's *New York Herald*:

> *Captain G.M. Edgett of the late ship Charles Dennis wishes, through the columns of your paper, on behalf of himself and crew, to publicly express his heartfelt thanks to Captain Curtis and crew of ship Belle of Bath for saving them from their sinking ship off Cape Horn at a great risk and danger to themselves, and also for very kind treatment received on board Belle of Bath till landed at Rio de Janeiro.*

In 1891, Curtis of the *Belle of Bath* heroically saved the crew of the *Charles Dennis* as it foundered off of Cape Horn. In 1899, along with his cousin Captain Frank A. Curtis and Alvah Treat, another Searsport resident, Curtis went to Alaska in search of gold but returned after a year. He was still a captain as late as 1928, the year he died. Curtis's former ship the *Tillie E. Starbuck* went down off of Cape Horn in 1907. Aboard it was Maine native Don Nicholson, who was serving as a mate.[122]

In 1853, in two small sailing ships stuffed with Maine workers and Maine lumber for buildings, William C. Talbot departed Machias for the Pacific Coast. He was captain of the fifty-ton schooner *Julius Pringle* on this 171-day voyage, which included several days of miserable weather off of Cape Horn. Talbot established a sawmill in Puget Sound in July 1853. By 1868, its name was changed from Teekalet to Port Gamble. The clipper schooner *L.P. Foster* accompanied them and carried mill machinery and merchandise for their store. It, too, suffered dreadfully at Cape Horn, but both successfully made the passage. The Port Gamble Mill, originally staffed by Mainers, operated continuously until 1995.[123]

The *Fresno*, a 160-foot 1,244-ton schooner built in Bath in 1874, spent years working Atlantic ports. It finally rounded Cape Horn to be reconfigured as a barge for the Alaska trade. Purchased in 1914 by North Pacific Sea Products, the *Fresno* carried whaling supplies from Seattle to Alaskan whaling stations at Akutan, then returned with whale oil or fertilizer back to Seattle. Brought to Lake Washington in 1920, it was laid up at Bellevue, where many whaling ships moored in the off season. It worked as wharf-side support until it caught fire and sank in 1923. The Sewall-built ship *Oriental* also ended its days in Alaska. After a distinguished deep-water career in the West Coast lumber trade, it went to the Alaskan salmon-packing fleet. The *Oriental* freighted men, supplies and canned salmon out of Alaskan waters until 1925.[124]

The 202-foot long 1,611-ton *Ivanhoe* was built in 1865 by C.P. Carter for wealthy Belfast businessman P.R. Hazeltine. Belfast native Edward Horace Harriman was its master. Launched on September 21, 1865, it went to New York to load for a San Francisco run. They departed on January 26,

Oil painting of 1864 Belfast-built ship *Ivanhoe* by marine artist and Belfast resident Percy Sanborn. *Courtesy of the Belfast Historical Society and Museum.*

1866, and doubled Cape Horn in the first week of April. Edward Mitchell, a sixteen-year-old passenger, kept a journal. Using the nickname for Cape Horn, Mitchell wrote on the first day of April, "I guess we are sure of a five months' voyage in the least, here we are at sixty-three days out, and we are within ten degrees of Cape Stiff." Two days later, he noted the cold and how they needed every piece of clothing to keep warm. By April 8, they were off the Horn.

> *This A.M., about nine o'clock, we made Cape Horn, and at half past ten we past* [sic] *it.... It is a small island rising up to a high bluff at the water's edge, and a small white rock in the shape of a hay cock just outside of it. It is a rough-looking place all around here.... We run up to it with topmost studding sail and Royals set.... We had not past more than a half an* [hour] *before we had her under reefed topsails, although we have had very fine weather for the latitudes. Our boatswain says that this is the twelfth time he has doubled Cape Stiff, and it is the best weather that he has seen here. We passed within about four miles of it; well, we are around the first corner and half the distance passed over, but it took a long time to do it, seventy-two days.*[125]

Even with a good rounding of Cape Horn, they were not free of danger. The following day, Mitchell noted:

> *We had a very narrow escape from going ashore on Diego Ramires Islands, at dark, we could just see them to leeward, they being very low land and it was very dark and the sea running high, we could not see them; as luck would have it, about three o'clock, the moon came out, and there was Mr. Islands just under our lee; we got the ship on the other tack as quick as we could and set the fore lower topsail, we just cleared them, and that was all you could say about it, for there was no room to spare; if we had struck, there would not have been one of left to tell the tale.... The mate caught an albatross today that measured eleven feet from the tip of one wing to the tip of the other.*[126]

On April 12, he wrote, "I think we shall have to go around Cape Horn again, as I think we have drifted to the easterd [*sic*] of it." The following day, he recorded:

> *In the morning, we had a heavy squall and it was cold to* [sic], *by the time a man got aloft he would not know whether he had hold of a rope or not.... Passed Cape Horn for the third time. This P.M., tacked two or three times; here we have been ever since last Sunday, getting nowhere.*[127]

On April 17, he recorded, "All us boys do is to stand by halyards, night and day, cold job in a hail squall." He noted they had to round Cape Horn multiple times, as easterly winds drove them back. Heavy seas also caused the ship to lurch; he described one swell that cleared all the pots and kettles off the galley stove, so everyone missed their dinner. On April 21, Mitchell sighted floating wreckage, two water casks and part of a ship's house. Two days later, he wrote, "Last night, it blew very hard, she took a sea in that filled the decks nearly full and like to washed a man overboard, notwithstanding she is a very dry ship....This P.M., I have been picking Albertross [*sic*] in the cabin. The wind has been very moderate all day." For the rest of their time in Horn waters, Mitchell noted that the harder the winds blew, the less sleep they got.[128]

The *Ivanhoe* earned notice when it carried 180 immigrants to Sydney, Australia. It then went to coaling on the West Coast, where it was owned by the Black Diamond Coal Company. In September 1894, the thirty-year-old worn-out vessel went missing after leaving Seattle. Loaded with

coal, two male and two female passengers and a crew of eighteen, it had started for San Francisco. Lost in a gale, the wreck was never definitively found until a Willipa Bay lighthouse keeper's wife found buried in the sand a nameboard that said "Ivanhoe" in large letters. An oil-on-linen painting of the *Ivanhoe* was done in 1870 by well-known maritime artist and Waldo County native Percy Sanborn. Sanborn, born in 1849, moved to Belfast and became a house, sign, portrait and landscape painter. He kept a collection of cardboard profile patterns for the vessels he had painted, including the *Ivanhoe.* Known as a Renaissance man, Sanborn also wrote poetry, composed music and conducted an orchestra. He died in 1929 after being struck by a taxi while leaving the Belfast Free Library.[129]

Another Bath-built down-easter to engage in Cape Horn trade was the 1,849-ton *A.J. Fuller.* Launched in May 1881, the ship was commissioned by New York's Flint & Company and built by John McDonald. Rigged with a billet head, it had three decks, three masts and had a length of 229 feet. When compared to earlier clippers, the *AJ. Fuller* carried only 28 crew members; meanwhile, the same-sized clipper ship *Sovereign of the Seas*, just twenty-five years earlier, had required a 108-man crew. Its first eleven years, the *A.J. Fuller* was commanded by Searsport-native Captain Theodore P. Colcord. Born on December 13, 1848, he died on March 22, 1914. Colcord used the *A.J. Fuller* for fast shipments from New York to San Francisco and Liverpool; its main challenge was doubling Cape Horn. An 1882 handbill advertised the *A.J. Fuller* as a "magnificent A-1 first-class clipper ship," but it was actually a large down-easter. In October 1889, it was sold, and it spent next three decades working in the Pacific Northwest. Its captain was Searsport native Henry Nichols of *Patmos* fame. The *A.J. Fuller*'s end came on October 30, 1918, when the steamship *Mexico Maru* collided with it in dense fog. The down-easter sustained a 10-foot hole in its bow and rapidly sank. On June 24, 2000, a team of local divers in Elliott Bay, Washington, tentatively identified the wreck.[130]

Felix Reisenberg was one sailor who doubled Cape Horn aboard the *A.J. Fuller* under Captain Nichols. He, too, became a captain and published a book in 1950 titled *Cape Horn.*[131] Of note is his description of being a young, able seaman rounding the Horn in a storm.

> *For a week past, it had been growing colder and colder. The sea, seldom quiet in those latitudes, kept the ship lively; frequent shifts of wind, always strong, made constant work at the braces, between our spells at the bilge pumps, for water was working into her with the regularity of fate. Seldom*

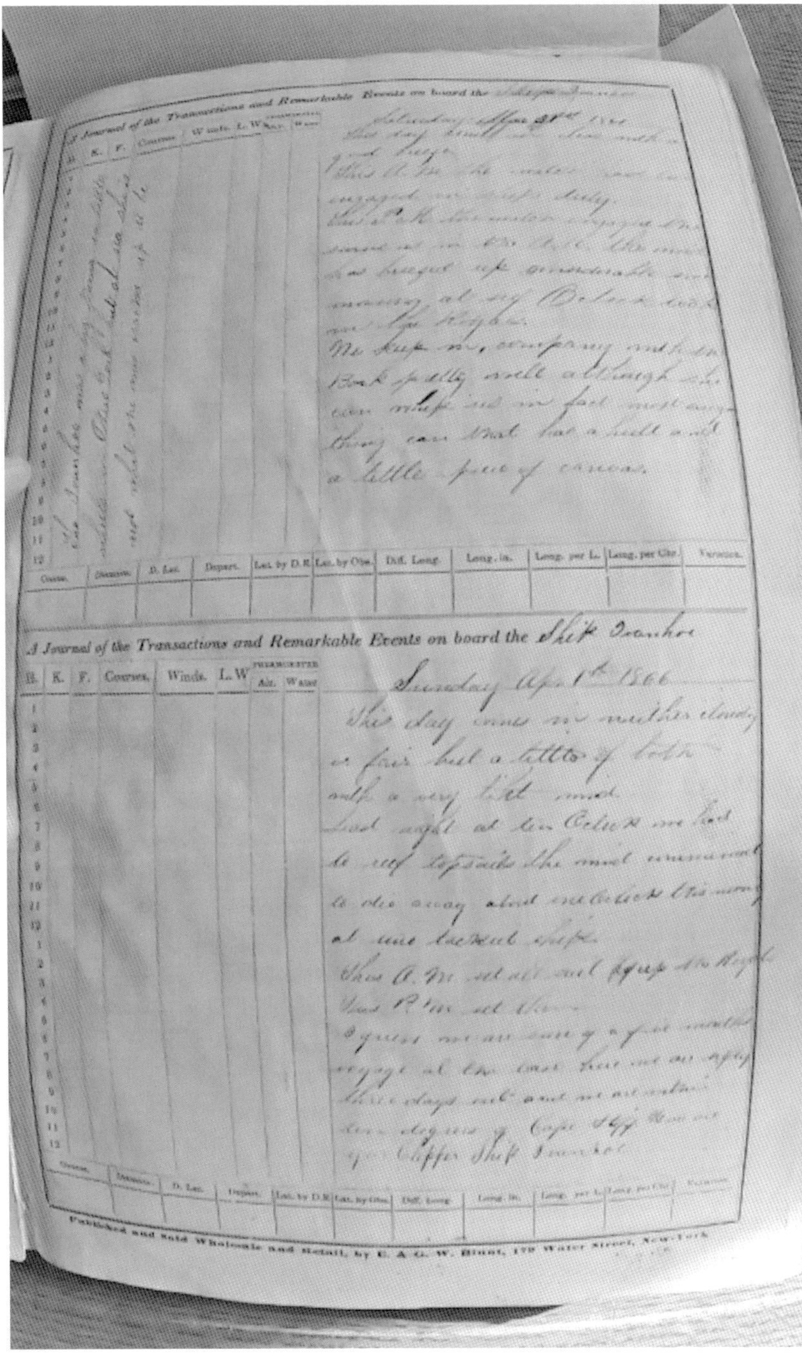

Logbook of *Ivanhoe*. *Photograph by Charles H. Lagerbom, from the Penobscot Marine Museum.*

> *did the pumps suck until six bells. Only when the working of gear kept us from pumping would the watch go by with that back-breaking labour.*[132]

Riesenberg wrote that the weather turned for the worse, so he was not surprised when his port watch crew were awakened in the middle of the night with a mate roaring at them, "All hands on deck! Out! Every mother's son of a bitch! Out you go!" They hustled past the mate and into a wild world of water, spray and motion. Riesenberg noticed that the sails overhead were thrashing and thundering, but any noise was lost in the confusion of storm.

> *Hang on! Oh! God! My mouth was full of salt water. Black, cold seas—solid ocean was lifting us, sweeping the gang along the lee side of the house, into the waist. Running ropes streamed across the deck. The water was filling our oilskins, our boots, wetting our shirts up under our armpits. The slippery deck rose, and she scended to windward, hitting us, knocking us down. Another flash, followed by close, reverberating thunder, deadened our hearing. The white fire has, for an instant, lit a picture of indescribable confusion and speed.*[133]

Riesenberg recognized the mate's roaring voice ordering them aloft to secure mainsails. Six men hauled themselves up flat against frozen rigging into the "black pandemonium of the night." Whipped by hail, they climbed. Edging out onto icy footropes, they desperately held on to the spar with interlocked frozen fingers as it wildly swayed back and forth.

> *Cold bodies were forgotten. Fingernails were broken off and bleeding, no one knew. We smothered the bulge of the sail.... The screaming of the wind and the cut of sleet were our thunderous applause; the mighty tossing of the ship, exaggerated because of our height, gave grandeur to our victory. We had saved the topsail!*[134]

5

HIGH RISK, HIGH REWARD

I did blow away my share of sails.
—Captain Charles Melvin Nichols

The reward of successfully doubling Cape Horn was often countered by the possibility of delay, damage or disaster. According to one sailor:

> *Because of its extreme weather, the ice and boisterous seas, Cape Horn takes precedence over other great capes as the headland of hazard. Seaman talk of it along the water fronts of the world. Not to have sailed around the horn is equivalent to not being a sailor. Seldom does the horn fail to live up to its evil reputation.*[135]

Portland's *Butler* was built in 1850 and was owned by Charles R. Green of New York. It sailed for San Francisco in July, right after launching, under Cape Elizabeth native Captain Silas D. Greg. Just short of Cape Horn waters, the *Butler* went ashore in fog at Cape San Antonio in southern Argentina. Greg and his family eventually reached Buenos Aires and safely arrived back in Maine on March 27, 1851.[136]

The Rockland bark *Jenny Pitts* was built in 1852. Two years later, it doubled Cape Horn while carrying a load of coal from Cardiff, Wales, for San Francisco. The *Jenny Pitts* faced heavy seas off the Falklands and spent twenty-four hours battling west-northwest gales off the Horn. From

San Francisco, it continued on to Hawaii, then to Hong Kong and around Cape of Good Hope to complete its circumnavigation. The *Jenny Pitts* eventually ran aground in Hawaii and was a total loss. Another Rockland ship, the *John Cottle*, built in 1854, saw a decade of Cape Horn service until it burned and sank at Valparaiso. It was intentionally burned by its crew, who told stories of harsh treatment by the captain, such as being locked in the forecastle every night. Another Rockland ship, the 1855-built *Oliver Jordan*, encountered heavy weather off of Cape Horn in October 1860. Captain John Robbins reported extensive damage and a bad leak. Most of the crew members proved useless due to extreme cold and exposure. In trying to make Uruguay, the *Oliver Jordan* foundered forty miles from Cape St. Mary. The crew took to three boats; one immediately capsized. Robbins and a dozen men survived after reaching a sandbar in the Rio Grande.[137]

The Lubec-built 193-ton brig *Cardin* (or *Carolyn*) *H. Kennedy* was launched in 1853. Its master, thirty-four-year-old Captain James Randall of Cutler, died aboard while off Staten Island, near Cape Horn, in December 1859. His remains were shipped home to Cutler for burial.[138] Kennebunk native Captain George W. Nowell sailed the *Tropic* around the Horn to San Francisco in 1860. In heavy fog on its return voyage, the *Tropic* was involved in a collision. Nowell reported:

> *Her jib boom went through our foresail and main topmast staysail; it broke short off and remained on board with everything attached, and the bark went clear. We shortened sail and hove to and laid by 12 hours. At noon the next day, the weather was clear and nothing being in sight from aloft, filed away and proceeded.*[139]

Nowell then encountered the Franklin-built schooner *Potomac* in distress. He was able to haul in its captain and three crew members amid very heavy seas. But Nowell's luck ran out in 1862 during a run from Philadelphia to San Francisco. With a load of coal and twenty-one sailors, the *Tropic* sailed into oblivion, never to be seen again.[140]

Two brothers, both fifth-generation captains from St. George, met up while off of Cape Horn. They had not seen each other for nine years. In Baltimore, where each ship had loaded coal for San Francisco, they had just missed each other. Captain Edward Watts and the *Pactolus*, a Thomaston bark built in 1865, were partially dismasted in a hurricane in the far South Atlantic. Once off the Horn, the winds dissipated. A nearby vessel, also becalmed, turned out to be the *John McDonald* under command of his

Watts family monument, Elmwood Cemetery, Thomaston, Maine. *Photograph by Charles H. Lagerbom.*

brother Captain Seymour Watts. For four days, they sat idle with three miles of water between them. Seymour signaled that he wanted to visit, and a ship's boat was lowered. His wife chose not to go, and Seymour spent a few hours chatting with his brother. Watts returned to his ship, and a few hours later, a terrific gale hit, separating the vessels. Edward Watts and the *Pactolus* arrived in San Francisco, but the *John McDonald* and Seymour Watts were never seen again. Edward Watts was sixty-nine years old when he died in 1913. He was buried in Elm Grove Cemetery in Thomaston.[141]

This Thomaston bark *Pactolus* may have been involved in the story of a lost Cape Horn island. In 1885, the vessel was commanded by William Dixon Burnham. At 4:00 a.m., while about 250 miles west-southwest from Cape Horn, Burnham noticed the sea had turned thick and yellow. This continued for thirty miles. He sounded and found black sand and small rocks at 68 fathoms deep, or 408 feet, while the surrounding depths were over 1,000 fathoms deep. This seamount, now known as Pactolus Bank, may have been an "island," one that Francis Drake may have sheltered on rather than Cape Horn Island. Polar explorer Admiral Richard E. Byrd searched for it with the USCGC *Bear* at end of his

1939–41 United States Antarctic Service Expedition. The name for the bank, however, may have come from another vessel named *Pactolus*; this one was built in Nova Scotia and was lost in the vicinity. Argentine sailor Piedra Buena, famous for rescuing mariners off of Cape Horn, was instrumental in saving men from a ship named *Pactolus* in 1882, but that vessel was from Nova Scotia. To further confuse matters, a later 1,674-ton Maine clipper named *Pactolus* was designed by John McDonald and launched on September 21, 1891. It was one of the thirty McDonald-designed ships built in Bath, and it also engaged in the Cape Horn trade. As for Pactolus Bank, further searches have not found anything; it has been designated as one of those mysteries at sea.[142]

Another Thomaston connection with the Horn is Captain William J. Willey's ship *Alfred D. Snow*, a three-deck ship built in Thomaston by Samuel Watts. Launched on May 17, 1877, the 232-foot ship made its maiden voyage in July 1877 and rounded Cape Horn that October for a 125-day run to San Francisco. For the next ten years, it made eight westbound and seven eastbound Horn runs. The crew of the 1883 voyage included his wife and two daughters, but it proved to be so stormy in Horn waters that they refused to accompany him on his next voyage. They got beyond Cape Horn, but then a gale hit, their cargo shifted and they were forced to hove down for six hours, with considerable damage done about the decks and in the cabins. They lost the foreyard and several sails in a very heavy gale. The run ended up taking 136 days. A second storm just after their doubling of the Horn blew them so far off course that they stopped at Pitcairn Island for repairs. While there, pieces of the HMS *Bounty*, which was burned in the harbor, were presented to the Willeys. During that same voyage, a sailor made a ship model of the *Alfred D. Snow* and presented it to Willey's daughter Lizzie. The Maine Maritime Museum holds an 1886 oil painting by William Howard York of the *Alfred D. Snow*; in it, the ship is depicted as being reefed down for heavy weather off the Horn. It sailed the triangular Cape Horn route from New York to San Francisco for wheat, and then it went on to England before going back to New York.[143]

Cape Horn voyages are filled with Maine heroics and stories of rescue. In 1868, Maine captain Edgar Chase took his new bride on a honeymoon voyage to Peru aboard the Damariscotta-built *Jonathan Chase*. The main part of its cargo was a huge locomotive engine, the first of its kind bound for Peru. Too big for the hold, it was lashed to the deck. Such a heavy load high on its decking compromised the *Jonathan Chase*'s center of gravity, making the ship roll fiercely while off the Horn, a constant threat to turn turtle or

A ship model of *Alfred D. Snow* made during a Cape Horn voyage for the captain's daughter Lizzie. *Courtesy of the Thomaston Historical Society.*

capsize. They barely survived the passage, and upon their arrival in Peru, Chase and the crew were kept from unloading the locomotive for weeks by local natives who would not allow it off the ship. They protested the locomotive, calling it a black devil.[144]

In May 1883, the Thomaston-built bark *Minnie M. Watts* sailed from New York to Portland, Oregon, with Thomaston-native Edwin Watts as its captain. Its cargo consisted of steel rails and railroad car wheels. By July 22, they were east of Cape Horn and had been spoken to by the Thomaston ship *J.B. Walker*. A British ship reported a vessel of the *Minnie M. Watts*'s description disappearing into atrocious weather to the west. The bark was never seen again. The *Minnie M. Watts*'s captain, his wife, his son as mate and two daughters were all lost. A remaining son who had stayed behind for schooling became the sole surviving family member.[145]

Searsport captain James Pendleton Butman delivered his daughter Margaret Elizabeth Butman to the *Elizabeth* while it was off the Falkland Islands in March 1887. Searsport native Captain James Gilmore Pendleton's twenty-two-year-old son, James Locke Pendleton, was killed

off Cape Horn when he fell from the rigging while serving as a mate on the *Elizabeth*. After surviving Cape Horn, Searsport native Captain Horace Seaver Clifford of the bark *Neried* died twelve days out from Valparaiso. He was buried at sea. Worse, the bark became a total wreck when it was driven ashore only one day after its arrival. Another Searsport native, Captain Edward Dean Blanchard, was in command of the *R.R. Thomas*. In 1897, while sailing from Hong Kong to Boston, Blanchard suffered an apoplectic stroke off of Cape Horn. The ship tried to reach the Falklands, but contrary winds kept them off. By the time they reached Montevideo, Blanchard was dead. He was buried in the small English cemetery in town.[146]

The Bath-built *William P. Frye* took a cargo of sugar from San Francisco to Delaware in 1903. Its captain reported that its rudder needed adjustment, as it steered badly while off the Horn. In fact, he wrote that they nearly broached in a Cape Horn snorter, but they made the passage; one sailor was lost overboard. In 1908, the *William P. Frye* sailed for San Francisco and was battered by Cape Horn storms for nearly four weeks. One sailor had been lost while on the plunging bowsprit. Constant storms shifted the ship's cargo and allowed no navigational sights to be taken for eleven days. They finally hove to in thick fog, and Captain Murphy ordered the men to sleep in their clothes in case they had to abandon ship. At this point, breaking surf was heard. According to one sailor, Murphy spotted land and disappeared below while mates got the ship around a small island with so little canvas showing—the sailor considered it a wonderful display of seamanship. But the *William P. Frye* was then committed to drifting through the islands, which it successfully did for nearly twenty miles. They tried to ascertain their position but were unable to do so until they drifted clear of land and the weather moderated. Everyone seemed in a dazed state of wonderment at their survival.[147]

The Bath-built *Samaritan* rounded Cape Horn in November 1863 as part of the Peruvian guano trade. Woolwich native Captain Frank Stinson reported losing two men and badly straining the ship while making the doubling. Instead of a compulsory examination and expensive order by authorities to re-caulk the *Samaritan*, Stinson settled the issue with a $300 bribe. In August 1872, the Sewall-built ship *Eric the Red* reached the Peruvian guano grounds after having lost a man off of Cape Horn. Another Sewall connection was Captain Joseph Small of the *Thomas M. Reed*. He had been severely hurt in a fall he suffered while rounding the Horn; he never fully recovered.[148]

The Sewall ship *El Capitan* was launched in 1873 in Bath and was sold to New York owners in 1884. In January 1883, two men fell to the deck from

Ship model of Cape Horner *El Capitan. Photograph by Charles H. Lagerbom, from the Penobscot Marine Museum.*

its rigging while off of Cape Horn. One later died, and the other was laid up for the rest of the voyage. Another sailor broke his arm during the passage. In 1897, the *El Capitan* departed Baltimore with coal for San Francisco and faced hurricane-force winds off the Horn, which shifted its cargo and destroyed the cabin. It took two weeks to make the repairs and right the ship, at which point, they limped into Montevideo, where the vessel was condemned. On that final passage, the *El Capitan* had also lost two sailors while in Horn waters, but this was not due to weather. One died of syphilis, and the other died of tuberculosis. Searsport's Penobscot Marine Museum displays a full model of the *El Capitan*. For years, the model was used in court cases in Portland, many involving at-sea collisions.[149]

A sister ship of the *Shenandoah*, the Sewall-built *Rappahannock*, sailed with a load of coal from Liverpool to San Francisco in July 1891. For forty days, Captain Wiley Rogers Dickinson, his family and the crew battled Cape Horn weather. They actually passed the Horn three times, only to be blown back to the east. Most of *Rappahannock*'s sails were shredded. After eventually passing the cape, Dickinson found his cargo of coal on fire, a case of spontaneous combustion. He quickly made for Juan Fernandez Island off of Chile. At Cumberland Bay, they saved stores, but an explosion midship, followed by another, doomed the vessel. It burned quickly and

sank in six fathoms. The refugees eventually landed at Valparaiso and were then transported on to San Francisco. A watercolor painting shows the ship's wreck on the shore, the sun setting in background. Written on the paper backing is a note from Dickinson's daughter: "We were cast away there on Robinson Crusoe's island for two weeks, Mother, Grace and I, (signed) Bessie E. Dickinson."[150]

No date was recorded for Searsport captain Charles Wesley Carr's death; he died at Cape Horn, near Staten Island. Captain John C. Blanchard II, one of many Searsport Blanchards, died while off the Horn in 1879. He was on the maiden voyage of *Wachusett* from San Francisco to Queenstown, Ireland. In 1888, Maine native Benjamin F. Carver II died of beriberi off the Horn while serving as the captain of the *Llewellyn J. Morse* on a voyage from Calcutta to New York. John Herbert Colcord reached San Francisco after a difficult cape doubling in 1891, only to be killed when his ship the *Elizabeth* broke into two on the rocks within sight of the city. The 1854 Thomaston-built clipper *Crest of the Wave* made multiple record runs from New York to America's West Coast. On one voyage off Cape Horn, the *Crest of the Wave*'s captain's wife, its mate and thirteen crew members died from yellow fever. Captain Joseph Hamilton of the Sewall-built Bath ship *Roanoke* died off of Cape Horn in 1897, apparently of blood poisoning.[151]

Phippsburg native Captain Samuel H. Morrison took the Sewall-built ship *Oracle* from San Francisco around Cape Horn in January 1883. As the *Oracle* neared the cape, it encountered a series of westerly gales that reached hurricane force. One sailor was swept overboard, and the *Oracle*'s wheelhouse and after-cabin were destroyed by wind and waves. Yarmouth native and a mate on the *Oracle* Omar Humphrey wrote, "Men were blown against the houses and held there, impossible to move. They could only drop on deck and creep and lash themselves to keep from being blown overboard. The ship lay on her beam ends with the water up to the hatches."[152]

When visibility allowed, the crew saw seas breaking against the cliffs close to their lee beam. Humphrey wrote they were saved by the cool actions of Captain Morrison. As the *Oracle* neared the breakers, Morrison ordered the wheel put up hard. The vessel miraculously slipped between towering cliffs on either side, into smoother water. Eddying currents, however, grabbed the ship and hurled it with tremendous force against a cliff wall. "Boats were then made ready, officered, manned, made fast to the ship....We had only time to secure a few clothes when our ship listed over and sunk entirely from sight, sliding off into deep water."[153]

Morrison and his crew reached an island eight miles north of Cape Horn, then spent the following week deciding their next course of action. The captain, Humphrey and five others decided to take their longboat through Strait of LeMaire to reach the Falklands, almost 360 miles away. Two days into this difficult small boat voyage, they were picked up by a German bark whose captain did not want to risk taking his ship for the other stranded men of the *Oracle*. Instead, he took them to Valparaiso, where Morrison organized his own rescue operation, which included Humphrey. All of the *Oracle*'s crew, though cold and hungry, were safely rescued.[154]

The worst Cape Horn loss for a Maine-built Sewall ship occurred in April 1906, with the loss of the steel four-mast bark *Arthur Sewall*. Built in February 1899, it was the pride of the company and its namesake owner. On its maiden Horn voyage, the *Arthur Sewall* leaked all the way from Cape Horn to San Francisco. It took six hours of pumping a day to keep them afloat. The rough passage had broken many of its copper over-the-pin rail joints. Captain Jim Murphy recommended in future that it carry extra pumps. However, more voyages saw more severe leaks, as well as rivets working loose. Another of *Arthur Sewall*'s captains wrote that he found, on close examination, he could turn many of the rivets around with his thumb and finger. In April 1906, Captain Thomas Burton Gaffry sailed the *Arthur Sewall* from San Francisco to Delaware by way of Cape Horn. The ship was never seen again, lost with all hands. It was believed that a massive structural failure had been the cause, aided by ferocious weather off of Cape Horn.[155]

In 1874, Frankfort native Captain Amasa D. Field buried his newborn daughter at the Falkland Islands after she died while they battled the waters off Cape Horn. In addition to burials, the damage suffered off the Horn often necessitated a visit to the Falklands. The Belfast-built bark *Ortona* was reported wrecked on the islands in 1855, when the vessel was seven years old. The 276-ton vessel had been built by White Connor Company. In 1899, Damariscotta native Captain Omar Chapman and the three-skysail ship *John R. Kelley* were also dragged onto the rocks of the Falklands.[156]

Cape Horn and the Falkland Islands are prominent figures in the life and death of North Haven native Captain Jesse Thayer Carver. In 1890, he did what many other sea captains of his time did—he gambled everything he owned on a single ship and its voyage. Deep in debt, he knew this one voyage would likely make or break him. The ship was the down-easter *St. Mary*, its destination was San Francisco and Carver was to be its master. His challenge was to get the large vessel successfully around Cape Horn and delivered to San Francisco on time.

The author doing research in one of Port Stanley's pubs; the poster behind is a complete visual record of known shipwrecks around the Falkland Islands. *Photograph by Jon Cox, from the Charles H. Lagerbom collection.*

The *St. Mary* was everything to him, and years later, others from his native state of Maine also recognized its value.[157]

Jesse Thayer Carver was born on March 26, 1833, into a Maine seafaring family. At an early age, he went to sea, becoming captain in 1861 at the age of twenty-eight. His first turn was as master of the brig *John Henry*. Before 1864, he became master of the brig *Harriet H. McGilvery* after marrying Evelina W. Nichols (1835–1913), who was also from a Maine maritime family. In 1882, he became the master of *Richard P. Buck* for next seven years, but that ship's career ended in disaster when drunken sailors set fire to it while it was at anchor in St. Georges, Bermuda, in the summer of 1889. The Bath-built 1,567-ton full-rigger was a total loss and considered a mark against Carver's name and reputation.[158]

His next and final ship was the down-easter *St. Mary*, which was launched from Charles V. Minott's shipyard in Phippsburg. The *St. Mary* was 242 feet in length, 42 feet wide and 18 feet deep. Its keel and frame were made of white oak and timbers of yellow pine. Launched on March 20, 1890, into the Kennebec River, the *St. Mary* was described as "majestic." Local papers

stated, "The launch was a beauty; she is a remarkably built vessel, the best frame ever seen around these parts."[159]

Captain Jesse Thayer Carver. *Courtesy of the Penobscot Marine Museum.*

By 1890, large wooden sailing ships like the *St. Mary* were considered risky investments to build, own and operate, especially with rise of steam-driven vessels and British-built steel hulled craft. Even Minott's own son, Charles Jr., the heir to the business, recognized that times were changing. But Minott Sr. felt fortunes could still be made. The *St. Mary* cost $159,000 to build, and as it slid into the spring-swollen Kennebec River, Charles Minott Sr. held the largest number of its shares. His son and two daughters each got 1/64, while Carver also held substantial interest; one source thought it more than a quarter. At the age of fifty-seven, Carver wagered everything on the *St. Mary* and its upcoming voyage. Success would set him in comfortable retirement with his family back in Searsport. On January 13, 1890, Carver handed Minott Sr. a check for $12,000—his life savings. When the *St. Mary* left under tow for New York City that April, Carver owned a fourth of the vessel, yet he still owed Minott another $10,000. They agreed on a note that the debt would come due in December 1890, after the *St. Mary*'s voyage. Carver had nine months to make good on this financial roll of the dice.[160]

After arriving off the coast of New York May 3, the *St. Mary* was towed to South Street on Manhattan's Lower East Side for a final fitting out and cargo loading. A week later, five hundred tons of steel rails came on board. A week after that, ten tons of coal arrived. By May 20, Carver noted that the *St. Mary* had taken on some water and lamented they did not have an engine to power its pumps; it would have to be done manually. Most of the crew had arrived by May 29; agent T.F. Alexander charged $1,000 for shipping the crew. On May 30, the tug *American Standard* towed the *St. Mary* out beyond Sandy Hook to begin its maiden voyage to San Francisco. Papers in Minott records include a small bill receipt from the tug, signed by Carver to boatman Thomas Bresnan. The charge was $3.[161]

The *St. Mary* also carried whiskey, iron piping, boxes of tacks and metal toy trains for Christmas in San Francisco. Its crew numbered about twenty-

St. Mary at the docks in New York City, 1890, prior to its maiden voyage. *From the collection of Eric Berryman.*

five, including Carver; a mate, or chief officer; a carpenter; a steward; and a stewardess. The steward had arrived at Phippsburg with Carver the second week of April; his name was Clark. For fifty-seven days, the weather held fair and the *St. Mary* proved to be swift on the water. Carver recorded reaching twelve knots. On August 6, as they neared Cape Horn, the *St. Mary* overtook another Minott vessel. The *James Drummond* had departed from Philadelphia two weeks before the *St. Mary*, and Carver was pleased at his own down-easter's progress.[162] Unknown to Carver, the *St. Mary* was on a collision course with another vessel off of Cape Horn, the British ship *Magellan*.

In fact, there were at least ten other vessels in the vicinity of one another and Cape Horn that night. Nine were on the port tack, making their way slowly northward. The *St. Mary* had not yet come about and bore down on them, all battling westerly winds. The *St. Mary* was 130 miles west of the Diego Ramirez Islands, which lie 65 miles west-southwest of Cape Horn. While it was nighttime, there was moonlight, and the seas were relatively calm for wintertime off of the Horn. Still, conditions were such that Carver's decision to turn in for a spell that night was seen as partially responsible for what happened.[163]

Carver retired at midnight, but shortly after 1:00 a.m., he was called by the mate with the words "Here's a fellow who won't keep off." Carver later wrote that he had no sooner gotten on deck when the *Magellan*'s jib-boom loomed over the *St. Mary's* main yard. At the same time, he saw the *Magellan*'s crew burning its danger signal—way too late. Filled with creeping despair, a hastily scrawled later letter to his wife noted, "Had I only known that he was a ship that could not be kept off, I could have got out of his way….This is one of the most stupid accidents that I ever saw." Carver knew that at the *St. Mary*'s speed of 7.5 knots, they could easily have maneuvered if there had been ample warning from the mate. Carver thought the man had likely been looking for something to eat instead and that the ship's lookout had sat smoking his pipe in some closet out of the cold.[164]

Regardless, the two ships came together in a tremendous crash. The collision crippled the *St. Mary*. Carver wrote, "We were run into by another ship and badly stove up. All the mizzen rigging on the port side is gone, and all the sails and the chain plates all gone, quarter stove in, mainsail and mainyard gone, and a lot of other things all cleaned out on the lee side."[165] What he did not say but instinctively knew was his financial gamble was in serious jeopardy, and his hopes had possibly been crushed, along with the battered side of the *St. Mary*.

The other vessel, the *Magellan*, actually fared worse. Reeling off after impact, it was quickly lost from view from the *St. Mary*, and it was soon

filled with water. Although the *Magellan*'s hulk was reported afloat days after the collision, it was determined that no crew members had survived. The German bark *Para* later reported, on August 12, that it had encountered a large quantity of the *Magellan*'s cargo of parafine cases, as well as a body lashed to a cabin door.[166]

The weather, which, by Horn standards, had been decent, then turned bad. The wind and waves picked up, and the stricken ship's crew toiled day and night on deck or at the pumps. Few got any sleep, even after the storm passed, as winds turned southwesterly, still shrieking through sail remnants and broken rigging. It took four days for the ship to make its way eastward, toward Port Stanley in the Falklands, Carver's only hope to save the vessel, or at least the cargo. By August 10, as the *St. Mary* neared its goal, an exhausted Carver sought some rest. At 5:00 p.m., he gave orders not to be disturbed and was not awakened, even when, later that evening, the ship's course was changed from east-northeast to north. The new heading pointed the vessel directly toward land.[167]

Around 8:00 p.m., the *St. Mary*'s carpenter told the mate that he thought land was near, but he was not believed. He then went aloft on the fore royal yard and saw a white line of breaking surf. After quickly descending, he once again alerted the mate, who once again disagreed. When urged to call the captain, the mate also refused. At some point, Carver emerged on deck and immediately ordered the helm about. The ship swung but was too late and struck, getting hung up on a partially submerged outcrop called Pinnacle Rock.[168] It was after 9:00 p.m., less than an hour after the carpenter's first warning. As the tide turned and went out, the *St. Mary's* fate was sealed. If Carver had hoped to salvage his finances by getting the cargo safely to Port Stanley, he then knew he was ruined, just five months after *St. Mary*'s launching.

Dawn's arrival presented a bleak scene. The falling tide wedged the *St. Mary* on the pinnacle, and surf began pounding the ship, which began to disintegrate. The crew decided to abandon the vessel and make their way, by boat, to the nearby Fitzroy settlement and then on to Stanley. But Carver would not go. As they prepared to leave, Carver refused to join them, declaring that, three times in his life, he had been in serious trouble, but this was to be his last. When the stewardess approached him in his cabin to once again plead with him to come with them, she claimed he had filled a glass with a reddish mixture and was preparing to drink it. Grabbing it, she emptied the contents, but Carver supposedly replied he would get more after they left; just what the drink contained is not clear. When they tried to

actually force him to the boats, Carver pulled a revolver, threatening to shoot the first man who touched him.[169]

Two days after the crew landed at Port Stanley, a working party returned to the *St. Mary* and found Carver's body. This was likely when Carver wrote a letter to his wife, portions of which were copied and survive in Minott records. The *St. Mary*'s carpenter reported that Carver was found with froth at his mouth, looking like raw cotton. Carver was buried in the local Stanley cemetery on Sunday, August 17, 1890, five days after his body had been discovered, attended by a large number of islanders. On the day before the burial, a local coroner's inquest concluded, "[Carver] came to his death by syncope failure of the heart, accelerated by great mental excitement and worry." Most sources remain noncommittal about the cause of his death—only a few suggest suicide. His remains were later sent to Montevideo and eventually returned to Maine. Jesse Thayer Carver was buried in Searsport's Elmwood Cemetery on February 22, 1892.[170]

The *St. Mary* was a total loss. It sat level on its keel, like a book on its spine, and soon broke in half down the middle, where three rows of deck beams pointed upward, the main deck and two lower decks. What was left of its cargo was easily reached. Within days, two schooners took off

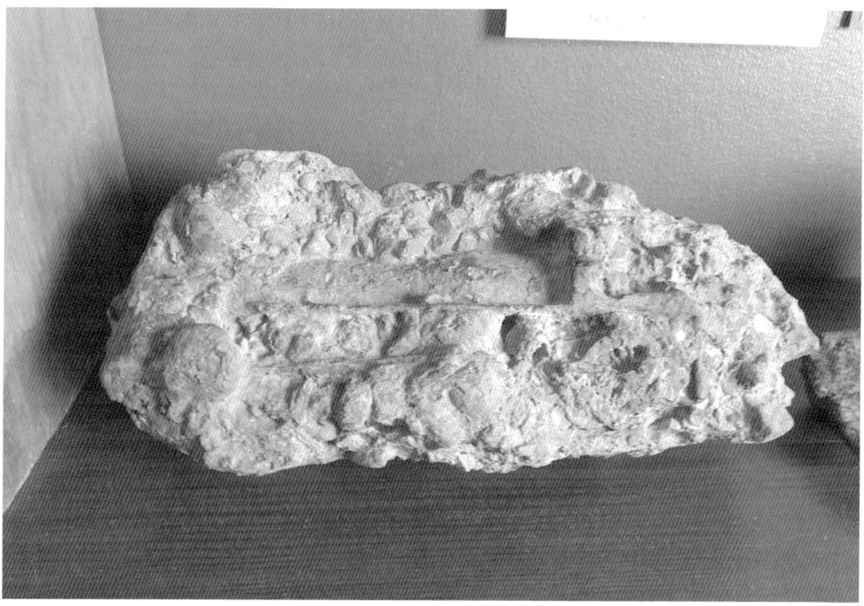

Concretion of metal toy train fragments from the *St. Mary* in the Falkland Islands Museum. *Courtesy of the Falkland Islands Museum and National Trust.*

quantities of coffee, whiskey, ink, soap and carpet. For years, the *St. Mary* was known locally as "the Christmas wreck" for its large quantities of toys. Many were metal toy locomotives, which spread holiday cheer to islander children that December.[171]

The mate, whom Carver blamed for the *Magellan* collision and whom the carpenter had warned about the ship's nearness to land, appears to have taken advantage of the situation for his own personal gain. An unsigned note that accompanied the papers from the vessel found at Stanley states that the officer was worthless and had stolen items from the wreck to sell. As mate, he was engaged by Lloyd's of London while on scene as an agent to look after the *St. Mary*'s cargo at a rate of two dollars a day. He apparently helped himself and sold off the binnacle. As the crew eventually departed, a warrant was issued for his arrest by the American consul, but nothing seems to have come of it; the man disappeared.[172]

Historical materials from the *St. Mary* were kept in the Charles V. Minott Shipyard Records, now housed at the Maine Maritime Museum Library in Bath. Box no. 157 contains twenty-five folders of *St. Mary* records, including its registration, insurance and construction materials and notes. Correspondence, accounts and a drawing of the incident can also be found, including a partial copy of Carver's letter to his wife following the collision; the original has not been found. With his cause of death determined as heart failure, Carver's widow received his life insurance and appears to have made good on the note to Minott Sr. Still, the loss of the *St. Mary* was a tremendous financial blow to Minott and his company. A year later, however, the company built the four-mast schooner *Merom* and then the ship *Aryan* in 1893.[173]

The story of the *St. Mary* did not end in 1890. For years, the down-easter sat on the rocks near Kelp Cove, thirty miles south of Stanley. The *St. Mary* quickly collapsed, its port side washed away into deeper water. During the 1970s, the *St. Mary* was remembered when Maine State Museum officials in Augusta wanted a locally built Cape Horn ship for its planned *Arts and Industries of Maine* exhibit hall. In 1977, a reconnaissance team traveled to the Falklands. Financed by the National Endowment for Humanities, they surveyed three different shipwrecks and found the *St. Mary* to be just what they were looking for. "*St. Mary*'s bones suited perfectly." Assisted by the National Maritime Historical Society, a salvage team under the supervision of maritime archaeologist Peter Throckmorton traveled to the islands in 1978 to bring back the *St. Mary* as a lasting symbol of the great role played by Maine in America's seafaring drama.[174]

Remains of the *St. Mary* in 2020, Whale Cove, Falkland Islands. *Courtesy of Ross James.*

The wreck lay partly awash near the Fitzroy and Bluff Cove settlements, eight hours away by jeep ride across "Camp," the roadless island expanse outside of Stanley. According to Throckmorton, this remoteness played a part in the *St. Mary's* survival, as it basically remained in a state of preservation due to the constant temperature and humidity. He argued

that the recovery of *St. Mary* was feasible at a nominal expense, since most of the needed equipment was already on hand and there were no further logistical challenges associated with the wreck, such as diving. The site was covered with scattered remnants from the ship and its cargo. As the *St. Mary* broke apart, its cargo washed ashore, including numerous cast-iron toy trains. Even today, a visitor can find, at low tide, rusty iron pieces of barely recognizable toys; a few still show some original color. Bits of original cargo lie everywhere, such as brown bottles of Buchanan's Whisker Dye and saddler's tacks in tied-up boxes.[175]

The task to physically return the *St. Mary* to Maine presented enormous logistical challenges. Many people and organizations stepped forward with assistance. The British Royal Marines on the island under Major Nigel Willoughby helped with the expedition camp, providing tents, arctic sleeping bags, primus stoves and field rations. A private ketch, then visiting the islands, was charted to ferry equipment to the site. Throckmorton and his crew established a base camp under the low bluffs on the beach near a colony of ten thousand Gentoo penguins. "The ketch *Jenny Wren* (built in 1926), en route from South Africa to English Harbour, Antigua, via a glimpse of the Falklands, was chartered to carry the saws, chains, and related fuels and spare parts from Stanley. There was crockery aboard marked 'Royal South Africa Yacht Club.'"[176]

The ketch's three-man crew also helped cut up the wreck and prepared hot meals at the end of the workday. A large section of the *St. Mary*'s starboard side had come ashore at Whale Point, while its masts, bowsprit and other pieces of wreckage lay strewn along six miles of rocky beach. The entire shore length was covered with wreck debris, such as turned stanchions, deadeyes, planks, frames, parts of spars and huge chunks of timber. One of the larger pieces was the ship's main beam. On it, the *St. Mary*'s official number from Minott's Phippsburg Shipyard was barely legible: 116317.[177]

Logistics member Eric Berryman reported squadrons of cormorants lodged among wreck timbers, making it a challenge as crew worked cutting away portions of the vessel. Homelite Corporation donated large chainsaws for cutting the hull on predetermined lines. Their travel to the Falkland Islands was also quite a story. Captain J.H. Scott of Military Sealift Command was able to get them, as well as several barrels of silicon, aboard the fleet auxiliary USNS *Mirfak* in Leonardo, New Jersey, which annually circumnavigated South America, delivering munitions to allied navies. Norman Brouwer, a historian for New York's South Street Seaport Museum, got the chainsaws to the ship just before it sailed. Captain John

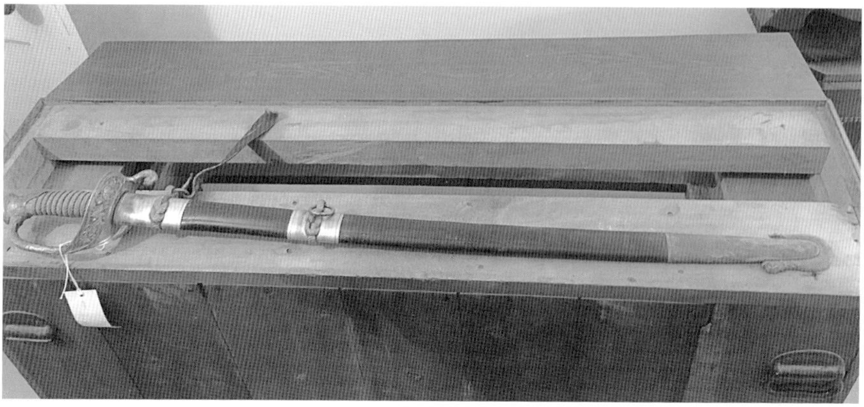

Above: The ceremonial sword of Captain Jesse Thayer Carver at Penobscot Marine Museum. *Photograph by Cipperly Good.*

Right: Metal toy trains from the wreckage of the *St. Mary*. *From the Eric Berryman collection.*

Arens, the master of the *Mirfak*, actually delayed the departure until Brouwer arrived with the saws. That equipment was nearly lost overboard when the *Mirfak* encountered heavy weather in the South Atlantic. The *Mirfak* finally arrived in Puerto Belgrano, Argentina. There, Argentina's navy stored the material until the naval vessel *Bahía Buen Suceso* made its annual run to Port Stanley. The chainsaws and spare parts were eventually delivered to Stanley by way of the Argentine Air Base at Comodoro Rivadavia in southern Patagonia. The silicon barrels followed aboard *Bahía Buen Suceso*.[178]

As the logistics officer, Berryman discovered that the far-south Falkland Islands had not been on any regular commercial freighting trade route for over ninety years. Ships rarely passed or stopped, making it a challenge to arrange any kind of return transport for the *St. Mary* pieces. A private

charter would be too expensive. "We needed a logistics bridge from the U.S. to the Falklands and back."[179]

A total of nearly thirty tons of remains were eventually recovered, twenty-two just from the hull section. Remaining pieces consisted of spars collected along the beach. The largest section, most of the *St. Mary*'s starboard side, lay flat against the beach, 130 feet long and 35 feet from pin rail through the main deck. Workers spent ten days sawing the hull; the entire operation spanned twenty weeks after months of planning. The result was ten numbered segments, each carefully measured 40 feet by 12 feet to fit the museum's designated space. The largest section, from between the decks, measured over 10 feet long and was dreadfully heavy. Throckmorton dubbed it "the beast." Some wanted to cut it up further, but the archaeologist refused.[180]

> *Iron fastenings in the hull were a constant menace to chainsaw operators as they tackled each section. The labor of cutting up the wreck was made harder by the unforgiving climate: winds of sixty knots and up and rain that could cut horizontally, playing tricks on focus, stripping muscles of their energy and endurance, and whittling away at our attention span.*[181]

Pieces were jacked onto a wooden sled, then laboriously dragged by tractor. They were skidded across land, over tussock grass, for more than two miles to a beach. The Falkland Islands Company had agreed to provide use of its freighter to transport sections from the beach to Stanley. Berryman remembered they skidded from Kelp Lagoon all the way to Pleasant Harbor. Peter Throckmorton, worried about the weight of "the beast," became alarmed when the tractor hauling it bogged down and stalled. With help from the interisland ferry M/V *Monsunen*, which was waiting a half-mile offshore, a line was brought to tow off pieces. In a steady rain, Throckmorton said they dragged lumps of the *St. Mary* offshore, "like giant sea turtles, one after the other." Berryman recalled large sections mostly bouncing along the bottom until they were alongside ship. They were then winched aboard.[182]

Eric Berryman's job was to get equipment to Port Stanley and bring the *St. Mary* back to Maine, absent any commercial transportation. While he was on hand to help with salvage, he credited Throckmorton with being the force of nature who successfully got twenty-two tons of the *St. Mary* to the Stanley Jetty. He recalled seeing Throckmorton overseeing the final pieces as they were winched off the beach, slowly over the seabed and then aboard the waiting ship. Throckmorton, referred to as father of underwater

The *St. Mary* salvage team taking a break from the incessant winds during the 1977–78 recovery expedition. *From the Eric Berryman collection.*

A Falkland Islands stamp depicting the *St. Mary* wreckage. *From the Charles H. Lagerbom collection.*

archaeology, died in June 1990 at his home in Newcastle, Maine, aged sixty-one.[183] "The St Mary is a monument in which I proudly share. It was a hell of an endeavor with gossamer-thin chances of succeeding. But succeed it did. Peter T. stands in the rigging above the exhibit, as he much deserves."[184]

At the Stanley Jetty, workers crated and hoisted pieces of the *St. Mary* aboard British Antarctic Survey vessel RRS *Bransfield*. Upon concluding its season, the vessel departed for Southampton, England. As it neared the United Kingdom, shipping agents McGregor, Dow and Holland announced a need for a deposit for landing and handling fees. They demanded $7,000 for pilotage, towage and berthing. Berryman noted the clear implication that British taxpayers were unwilling to pay anything to help with this American expedition. Financial concerns were eased when the Castine-based Maine Maritime Academy school training ship *State of Maine* volunteered to bring the *St. Mary* back on its way home from its annual cruise. Further, it was discovered that the *State of Maine* was still owned by the U.S. Navy, so it ranked as a visiting warship. This helped expedite matters and enabled it to berth at Her Majesty's Dockyard at Portsmouth, free of charge.[185]

Once in Southampton, carefully tagged pieces of the *St. Mary* were transferred to a Royal Navy landing barge under watchful eyes of royal engineers. Colonel P.K.A. Todd, commander of the Third Transport Group, used this tank landing craft to transport the *St. Mary* to Portsmouth, where it was transferred onto lighters and then handed over to the *State of Maine*. The training ship then brought the *St. Mary* across the Atlantic, back to Maine, eighty-eight years after its departure. Docking in Portland, Maine's National Guard 1,136th Transportation Company loaded pieces onto flatbeds and trucked up Interstate 95 to the state museum in Augusta. Once there, the recovered sections were reassembled under museum director Paul Rivard. Its entire transportation costs, likely worth a $500,000, had been provided at virtually no cost.[186]

The *St. Mary*'s pieces included some original cargo, hull planking, deck beams and a chess tree (this was a piece of oak bolted perpendicularly on the side of a sailing ship to help draw down and secure the clew of the mainsail). Larger *St. Mary* parts included two twenty-foot sections of a forty-foot deck rail and a worm-and-pinton steering mechanism. The large section was laid out end-to-end on the museum's floor. When measured, they were just five inches short from the specified forty-foot dimension requested in the original plan. Rivard said the total was an almost unbelievable perfect forty feet. "I am convinced that the section we presently have at the museum is within fractions of the original

The restored pieces of the *St. Mary* that were retrieved from the Falkland Islands and shipped to Maine to be placed on exhibit at Maine State Museum in Augusta. *Courtesy of the Maine State Museum.*

dimensions that you took on the beach." The resulting display weighed twenty-five tons.[187]

Such a project strengthened the historical ties between Maine, Cape Horn and the Falkland Islands. After the *St. Mary*'s return, Rivard received from the Falkland governor a large envelope with a wax seal embossed by his signet ring, something the museum director thought was right out of the nineteenth century.[188] During the expedition, miscommunications were rife, beginning with the team's unannounced arrival. There had been little forewarning to Falklanders, who were justifiably upset with no information being shared about a permanent removal of artifacts from their colony. Berryman noted:

> *There had been no explanation of who we were, what we were doing, or that we expected to take things away from the colony. I was the only*

> *member of the expedition to have brought official letters of introduction and deposited them with government house. Paul Barrish, the naval attaché in Buenos Aires had made a particular point of me doing that.*[189]

The standoff ended with the intervention of Frank G.G. Carr, the director of Britain's Greenwich National Maritime Museum, who smoothed things over and obtained the required permits.

The *St. Mary*'s return represents an acknowledgement of its historic value. The Maine State Museum now houses the most substantial example of a Maine-built, square-rigged down-easter in America, a veritable link with the history of Cape Horn. Its preservation costs were $15,000, mostly for preserving wood and arranging the hull section for display. The effort was truly international, with the State of Maine, the United States, the Falkland Islands, Argentina and Great Britain all involved, as well as agencies such as the National Maritime Historical Society and the World Ship Trust. Companies like Dow-Corning donated a half ton of expensive silicon to make molds of the fragile artifacts. Berryman's notes, papers and photographs of the expedition, as well as those of Peter Throckmorton, were deposited at the Maine State Museum in Augusta.[190]

For Eric Berryman, the expedition was an adventure:

> *The project represents the nearest thing I leave as a monument on earth. It's a collective remembrance of which I am only a part. Many people were involved, any one of whom for any reason could have ruined the outcome. Or caprice by the Antarctic Territory's notoriously unreliable weather might have struck us down. Not in another thousand years can so many individuals and events align themselves so perfectly. Evils besieged us that came in battalion-size strength, but we were allowed to prevail. And now there's a monument.*[191]

Thirty-four miles east of the museum and up Coastal Route 1, Jesse Thayer Carver's grave site sits quietly in a corner of a small cemetery in Searsport, not far from the water. The lichen-covered granite stone states "Died On Board Ship *St. Mary*." There is nothing about his battle with Cape Horn and subsequent shipwreck. Penobscot Marine Museum holds Carver's decorative sword, as well as six pieces from the *St. Mary*, including the shaft from the ship's wheel, six mast bands, two rigging cranes, a shackle and a dead eye.

The Falklands, Cape Horn and Maine are also connected by the Maine-built clipper ship *Snow Squall*. Launched at Cape Elizabeth in 1851 by Alford

Carver grave site in Searsport, Maine. *Photograph by Charles H. Lagerbom.*

Butler, the 742-ton ship measured 157 feet long and was painted white with a red-orange stripe along its gunwales. It sported a grinning dragon figurehead. On July 14, the *Snow Squall* slid into the Fore River Estuary and was sold to New York's Charles R. Green & Company for $30,000. Its "subsequent ports [were] dependent on the vagaries of market conditions." This delicate dance, waiting for cargo or a job, plagued the vessel, often resulting in costly slack time. Considered one of the fastest in the fleet, the *Snow Squall* saw general service for thirteen years. One captain was Cape Elizabeth native Silas D. Greg. Captain Isaac Bursley took the *Snow Squall* on its maiden Cape Horn voyage in 1852 from Boston to Honolulu. Owner Charles Green had determined the California boom had run its course. He was not alone. In 1849, 151 ships cleared Boston for San Francisco; the following year, 166 vessels departed. By 1851, however, only 35 ships cleared Boston for San Francisco. So, the *Snow Squall* headed for Hawaii.[192]

The clipper sailed on January 17, 1852, with a load of lumber, shingles, pickets and clapboards, as well as three passengers, two of whom were

Christian missionaries who were being sent to Pacific islands. They wanted to take Panama's shortcut for a faster arrival, but the church leaders who were footing the bill determined they needed the discipline of a Cape Horn voyage. The Horn did prove to be formidable, as they encountered high winds and poor weather and finally arrived Honolulu on June 2, 1852. Once back in New York, the *Snow Squall* sailed for San Francisco on February 24, 1853, with a load of flour, oats, starch and one hundred whiskey barrels. They logged 360 miles in a twenty-four-hour run, a very respectable fifteen-knot average.[193] "The *Snow Squall* experienced very severe weather on the passage. Was fifty-two days off Cape Horn, thirty-five of which were continuing heavy [seas] and driven as far south as latitude 60. Carried away all iron work of the bow sprit and steering apparatus, started channels, and sustained other damage."[194]

Back in New York, the clipper sat idle. Green tried the Rio de Janeiro trade, but by June 1856, he decided to send the *Snow Squall*, once again, to San Francisco. Weather off the Horn was atrocious, and the ship dismasted. In August, the captain recorded the *Snow Squall* taking on more water than usual. Off of Cape Horn, a gale slit its foretopsail. In quick succession, they lost main topmast, main topgallant mast, main topsail yard, maintop and main trestle trees. The crew spent several hours hacking at the tangle as it lay on deck and trailed over the side. As the *Snow Squall* swung wildly in the wind and wallowed in waves, the captain feared that the rigging banging against the ship's side might pierce the hull. After they were finally able to free the wreckage, they limped back into Montevideo for repairs before attempting the Horn once again. The *Snow Squall* arrived in San Francisco on January 31, 1857, after a voyage of 208 days.[195]

During the Civil War, the *Snow Squall* ran afoul of the Confederate raider *Tuscaloosa*, although the faster clipper was able to pull away from its pursuer and reached New York on September 14, 1863, with an exciting story to tell. The clipper was then showing its age and wear. Green was able to secure a cargo and dispatched it once again on a New York run to San Francisco. With a fresh coat of black paint and a white stripe in the between decks, the *Snow Squall* loaded tons of steamer lump coal, two hundred cases of alcohol and fifty cases of canned lobster. It also carried sixteen carboys of acid on deck and a sizeable quantity of explosives from Hazard Powder Company of Delaware. This last addition to the cargo had to be loaded safely in the harbor at Bedloe's Island. The *Snow Squall* departed on January 2, 1864. On February 24, it went aground at Tiera del Fuego while transiting the Strait of LeMaire near Cape Horn. Using

those straits saved more than a day's passage around Cape Horn and was choice of experienced captains. But this region, even in mid-summer, was treacherous with its "Stone Age geography" and unpredictable weather.[196]

In light rain and moderate wind, Captain Dillingham edged the clipper through the strait and reported at 1:30 p.m. that the wind came around to northeast while they were nine miles offshore. "At four PM, while still standing along shore, the wind suddenly died away and the current rapidly swept the ship in towards shore, so that in a few moments, and before her anchors could be made ready, she was carried forcibly upon the rocks at the entrance of the Strait of Le Maire, where she remained fast."[197]

Dillingham tried to heave the ship off the rocks with an anchor, but a sudden wind change caused the clipper to lurch and float free. A quick inspection revealed a damaged rudder and the hold full of water. They initially continued around Cape Horn but soon changed course to Stanley in the Falklands. Badly leaking, the *Snow Squall* limped into port. Dillingham discharged its cargo to ascertain hull damage. He also hired a local diving crew to check out the clipper's bottom while locals emptied its hold. Three weeks later, the leak was still not found. Problems rose with his idle crew, and Dillingham had his carpenter and cook jailed for mutiny. Rising costs, endless repairs and lost time all contributed to Dillingham's frustration. He arranged for another ship, the Freeport-built bark *Orsini*, to take his cargo on to San Francisco, and then he stripped the *Snow Squall* of all gear, auctioning it for $10,600. The vessel was condemned on April 23, 1864, and sold for $2,000 to the Falkland Islands Corporation (FIC). It was towed to its final resting spot near FIC's wooden jetty and left to rot in mud. In the meantime, Dillingham and the owner, Green, wrestled with bills, totaling over $16,000.[198]

As with the *St. Mary*, the *Snow Squall*'s story did not end there. In 1982, prior to the Falkland Islands War between Great Britain and Argentina, a reconnaissance team from Maine checked out the *Snow Squall*, the only example of an American-built clipper ship whose hull was known to still be in existence. Although the first sight of it was "mortifying," it was determined that parts might still be salvaged. Maritime archaeologist Peter Throckmorton found the clipper in three feet of water at low tide; the *Snow Squall* had been used as a pierhead fender for the island jetty. After World War II, piles had been driven through the vessel, and two others' hulks alongside it, which formed the foundation for the main island jetty at Stanley. Throckmorton suggested one silver lining to this situation was that vessel remnants had been covered in dirt and debris, providing

a good layer of preservation. The *Snow Squall* then lay heeled on its port side, perpendicular to the pier, which ran north–south. A large part of its port side was under the dock. Throckmorton reported that their initial dives were hampered by thick kelp, which covered the wreck and gave off a fine silt that quickly obliterated visibility. The bow was the most visible part remaining; its decks had long rotted away, as had any frames or planking subjected to daily tides. Throckmorton acknowledged the fact that the *Snow Squall* had been stripped, yet still noted very little original iron, strapping or copper. He associated such a lack to the economical aspect of its construction. Built quickly and cheaply to take advantage of the California Gold Rush era, the *Snow Squall*'s construction was almost too fragile for a ship that size.[199]

Over the years, the *Snow Squall*'s hulk had become a receptacle for trash. It was also struck by an oil barge during a gale after the reconnaissance team's visit. But restorers persevered and created a measured plan view drawing. They also wanted to take apart and bring back large parts of the vessel. More visits from the *Snow Squall* Project resulted in a two-ton section of the clipper being shipped in containers to Portland, Maine. By 1987, this state-led effort of successfully raising the *Snow Squall*'s bow and shipping it back to the state was completed. The clipper remains ended up at Bath's Maine Maritime Museum.[200] Its retrieval benefitted the history of the clipper ship era in general and clipper ship construction in particular. Like the *St. Mary*, the *Snow Squall* represents another great connection between Maine's maritime heritage and Cape Horn.

Captain Charles Melvin Nichols. *Courtesy of the Penobscot Marine Museum.*

Searsport native Captain Charles Melvin Nichols was born on January 20, 1851. He was captain of the Maine bark *Patmos* in 1876, when it loaded coal in Hull, England, bound for Valparaiso. The 739-ton *Patmos* had been built in 1859 in Bucksport by R.P. Buck and Company. It was 144 feet long, 30 feet in beam and 21 feet deep. Nichols was on his honeymoon with his new wife, Millicent Dow, the daughter of another Searsport captain. While off of Cape Horn, the *Patmos* had to be abandoned when it caught fire due to spontaneous combustion.

Icy, wet decks soon warmed with the heat, and the pitch began to melt, the oakum underneath having already burned out. Wooden hatch covers collapsed under the pounding of Cape Horn waves. A long boat was readied, and the crew gathered in the forecastle, waiting for Nichols to judge the seas and make the call. When it came, they hustled aboard and watched the *Patmos* settle into the water, icy waves battling the flames. With the vessel gone, Nichols, his wife and the crew steered northward, bailing for their lives. On the second day, they were rescued by a Liverpool iron vessel named *Pasithea*, or *Pretricia*, also bound for Valparaiso and also with a cargo of coal. Within hours of rescue, however, the weather turned worse, and the *Pasithea*'s captain lost his nerve. With no observations possible and a severe gale blowing, they faced a lee shore one hundred miles south of Magellan's Strait. The elderly English captain turned over the command to twenty-five-year-old Nichols, who used the combined crews to act quickly and save the ship. Charles Melvin Nichols died on April 5, 1937, in Searsport. A crewman of his once said Nichols never lost a spar on any of his future Cape Horn voyages. When he was told that, Nichols replied, "But I did blow away my share of sails."[201]

6

NO GOOD ALTERNATIVES

Below 40 degrees latitude, there is no law; below 50, there is no God.
—an old sailor saying

One option to avoid Cape Horn waters and the Drake Passage was to make for Magellan's Strait; at times, it was more accessible, although stiff westerlies were common in the narrow passage. The 350-mile waterway, only 2 miles wide at its narrowest, could quickly develop into a navigational nightmare. Dense fog and high winds, prevailing almost year-round, help create challenging and disastrous consequences for sailing ships. Contrary winds and gales could crush a ship just as easily as they could off the Horn. They could also slow a ship's progress enough to run short of water and provisions. Spanish explorers called the area Tierra del Fuego or "Land of Fire" due to its constant fog, as well as smoke from the constantly burning brush fires natives used to keep warm. An extremely inhospitable place, it is plagued with constant bad weather, hail and snow, as well as fierce unpredictable winds called "willawaws."[202]

The 259-ton Yarmouth-built bark *Abby Barker* discovered this when it became stuck in the straits for eighty days. Timothy Pratt had decided to take his family to California after their North Yarmouth home burned. His oldest son, Timothy Augustus Pratt, a Bowdoin College student, became the first mate, while his younger son Enos became the second mate. Pratt's wife and twin eleven-year old sons also went along. Stymied by fierce head winds, the *Abby Barker* finally won after nearly three months, only to have

Tierra del Fuego souvenir patch.
From the Charles H. Lagerbom Collection.

the senior Pratt drop dead on the deck. They eventually arrived Sacramento Bay, only to fall prey to a raging cholera epidemic, which claimed the lives of all onboard, except the twin boys, who eventually made their way back to Yarmouth.[203]

Charles Waite joined the brig *B.M. Prescott* as passenger when it sailed from Calais, Maine, on October 31, 1849. On their way to the California gold fields, Waite kept a journal describing a constant concern with a fellow passenger who turned out to be suicidal. By January 1850, they were slowly working their way through the straits and found the desolate waterway pretty much the same as when Magellan sailed through it 330 years earlier. One change, however, was the traffic they encountered. On January 30, they anchored in French Bay, just south of Port Famine. Waite noted that they were not the only ones in this barren corner of the world. In fact, they had been accompanied through the straits by numerous vessels. With progress so slow, Waite even had the opportunity to visit. He wrote, "This afternoon, I visited the ships that arrived today—the *Page* from Edgartown; the *Providence* from New York; and the *Flight* from Baltimore. Thus, I got to know that our voyage had been as fight as that of any of these.[204]

By the first week of February, the *B.M. Prescott* was still in the straits, fighting headwinds and still encountering more traffic. Waite wrote of the engrossing scenery, "The deep inlets and the high snowcapped peaks gave the small brig an insignificant appearance." Yet he added another steamer was seen that day.[205]

Some Mainers or their Maine-built ships never returned from these treacherous southern waters, and if they did, they were never the same. This was the case for Belfast captain and part-shipowner Edward Horace Harriman. In 1878, he sailed with his wife and son aboard the down-easter *P.R. Hazeltine*. At 1,836 tons, the 233-foot schooner was largest ever built in Belfast at that time. Constructed in 1875 by C.P. Carter for himself and Harriman, the vessel seemed ill-fated from the start. A load of Virginia oak crashed to the ground from a broken gaff in the first days of construction, barely avoiding harm to dozens of workers. Carter then became ill with Bright's disease and died before the vessel was completed. A week before launching, portions of the staging around the ship collapsed and four painters

fell over fifteen feet. A worker named Samuel B. Gillum was badly bruised. The *P.R. Hazeltine* was launched on May 25, 1876, although everyone had thought it would be named *C.P. Carter* after its late builder. But Harriman thought otherwise, deciding on *P.R. Hazeltine*, after prominent Belfast resident Paul Richard Hazeltine, a wealthy businessman and the original benefactor of the Belfast Free Library. On its very first voyage, the *P.R. Hazeltine* went ashore in thick fog at Cape Sable Island and had to jettison its deck cargo of timber. It was not strained, but its keel and planking were sorely chafed. Harriman reported the ship's compass was in error.[206]

Its next and final voyage was launched in December 1877, when they departed New York for San Francisco, with Harriman as master. His wife was aboard, as was as his twenty-year-old son, who was also his second mate. They encountered horrible weather when approaching Cape Horn. Harriman decided to seek shelter near the Wollaston Islands, a group of rocky bits of land in Nassau Bay, located between Cape Horn to the south and Navarino Island and Beagle Channel to the north. Most nineteenth-century sailing ships tended to stay away from the area unless weather was worse off of Cape Horn. That was the case in 1878, when the *P.R. Hazeltine* hit a submerged rock and sank in ten fathoms of inhospitable waters. Belfast newspapers first reported the *P.R. Hazeltine*'s loss in early April 1878. Harriman himself reported the ship had gone ashore near Cape Wollaston, Cape Horn, but that the vessel and cargo, worth nearly $500,000, were capable of being raised from ten fathoms. The cargo included 245 tons of coal, 200 tons of pig iron, 102 bundles of sheet iron, nearly 2,000 iron pipes, 75 cases of liquor, 586 barrels of whiskey, over a thousand kegs of nails, 3,500 cases of petroleum and 347 barrels of pickles. But by May, the newspapers reported that the ship was an entire loss.[207]

When the *P.R. Hazeltine* sank, Harriman, his wife and seventeen crewmen took to two boats and were later rescued by the French bark *Gustave*. Harriman's son took a third boat, which was quickly separated from the others in the horrendous weather. It was reported that Captain Harriman blamed the first mate for loss of the vessel. That May, Belfast's Mrs. George F. White received a letter from her son Wellington, who had been one of the *P.R. Hazeltine*'s crew members. It was posted from Portland, Oregon, where some of the *P.R. Hazeltine* crew had been taken by steamer from Valparaiso. White described them losing their fore top gallant mast just eight days out of port. As for the wreck, he wrote that they had been just a few miles from Cape Horn when Harriman decided

Belfast-built down-easter *P.R. Hazeltine. Courtesy of the Belfast Historical Society and Museum.*

to detour around Wollaston Island to avoid bad weather. At eight knots running, trying to round Wollaston, the *P.R. Hazeltine* struck a submerged rock. The next wave lifted the vessel and dropped it back onto the same rock, which holed its bottom and quickly put three feet of water in the hold. Within an hour, the first two boats were away, leaving the mate and seven others on board with a small boat. Avoiding local natives, the two boats struggled for the next eighteen days, facing privations from lack of food and horrible weather before finally being rescued by the *Gustave*.[208]

Harriman's son and six others were rescued in Straits of LeMaire by an American bark named *Sonoma* out of Boston, which transported them to San Francisco. For nearly two weeks, they had lived on mussels. At one point, they took shelter in a cave, only to find the remains of a boat, some oars, oil-skin clothing and skeletal remains. The skeletons, lying side by side, had no clothing on them and looked like their flesh had been stripped away. Suspecting cannibalism and sickened by the smell, Second Mate Harriman grabbed as much of the clothing as possible, as well as a box with fifteen pounds of tobacco, and fled back to the boat. He washed one of the oil-skin coats as best as he could to rid it of its fearful smell and also made use of a pair of large sea boots. According to later reports, the crew attempted to assert their authority a few times over Harriman as second mate but failed to do so. He kept control and sailed their small boat into LeMaire Strait, where they were picked up by the *Sonoma*.[209]

Other Belfast owners of the *P.R. Hazeltine* were notified by Captain Harriman in late May that the ship was in ten fathoms of water but could still be salvaged. He requested permission to draw the funds to do so, reckoning it could be successfully completed in five months. The other owners declined. Back in Belfast, Harriman made plans to return to Tierra del Fuego and salvage his ship; it became a driving obsession. He looked into chartering a sailing vessel, with eyes on the local Belfast barkentine *John C. Smith*. Harriman also got U.S. senator Hannibal Hamlin to contact the American minister in Chile, requesting the *P.R. Hazeltine* be protected until he got there.[210]

In September, it was reported that a visiting ship had found the *P.R. Hazeltine* entirely submerged. Some rigging was saved, and pieces were sent to the Punta Arenas governor. A month later, Harriman learned that potential rivals were interested in salvaging the ship and outfitting it at Montevideo, Uruguay. He feared their plan was to pillage his wreck. In January 1879, Harriman left for Cape Horn after engaging top salvage

E.H. Harriman's house in Belfast, Maine. *Photograph from the Penobscot Marine Museum.*

expert C.A. Jones of Montevideo. In the meantime, word surfaced that the ship *Kate Kelloch* had encountered natives in canoes near the wreck. Shots were fired, and three natives were killed. A warning was sent to Harriman to be on guard. In June, it was reported that he had made it to Cape Horn but was declared clinically insane, driven to the brink by anxiety and mental collapse. The reports of those who saw him in Montevideo confirmed the condition. At one point, he was taken to Havre for treatment. Newspapers finally followed the wishes of his family and refrained from further comment on his condition.[211]

The wrecker Jones visited the site and said that the *P.R. Hazeltine* was still in good condition. In January 1880, a report from Valparaiso announced that some of its cargo had arrived there after being salvaged, mostly barrels of whiskey and some pianos encased in tin. One diver on that salvage effort was known around Belfast. He was S.F. Purrinton, and he agreed with Herriman that the vessel could still be raised for a cost of about $15,000, but there were no takers. E.H. Harriman died in the Augusta, Maine mental hospital on August 14, 1893. His son Charles S. Harriman, the *P.R. Hazeltine*'s second mate, was the chief mate aboard the ship *Levi C. Wade* when that vessel was lost with all hands in 1884. Wellington White died in Miami, Florida, in 1937. Harriman's stately captain's home in Belfast was, at one point, a bed-and-breakfast notably called the Mad Captain's House.[212]

7

MORE THAN JUST A PASSAGE

No one is fit to judge a book until he has rounded Cape Horn in a sailing vessel.
—Van Wyck Brooks

The idea of doubling Cape Horn has assumed iconic status, at least in an artistic and literary sense. Paintings, songs, poetry, photographs and sketches abound about Cape Horn and its impact on sailors. Many Cape Horners memorialized their achievement with a tattoo of special design. A merciless place, British poet Rudyard Kipling wrote of "the blind horn's hate" in his poem "The Long Trial." Richard Henry Dana Jr. provided two accounts of his Horn passage in *Two Years Before the Mast*. His first visit was an east–west voyage (chapter 5), during which he took a spill down the mess stairs with the crew's meal when the ship made a sudden lurch off the Horn. During the return west–east trip (chapter 32), Dana experienced desolation but was cheered on seeing Staten Island, since it meant Cape Horn was behind them. In 1907, Jack London wrote his short story "Make Westing" based on his experience sailing from New York to San Francisco aboard Maine-built down-easter *Dirigo*. The gripping tale highlights the obsession to keep battling westward around the Horn.[213]

Cape Horn proved so dangerous, arbitrary and treacherous that it inspired belief in the supernatural. Many were convinced that spiritual forces, both good and evil, were at work. Aboard the *Bostonian* while doubling Cape Horn in 1856, Mainer Captain Moses C. Maling resorted to contacting spirits to find news regarding his dangerously ill daughter whom he left back in Kennebunk.

For several nights, spirits were called, and Maling learned his daughter had recovered. Maling also had to deal with evil spirits that intruded on his ship. Apparently, they took over Maling's medium during the seances, sixteen-year-old Henry Ward. Later a ship captain himself, Ward felt he had been instructed by spirits to throw a table across the room.[214]

Fighting their way off Cape Horn, Maling wrote:

> *The next day, after passing Staten Island, the wild winds of old Cape Horn came down upon us in full blast, and for 22 days, we encountered the most terrific weather. Snow and rain every day, and upon two occasions, our decks were completely filled with snow so that all hands were employed all day shoveling it off. After a hard battering of four weeks, we got around the horn into the Pacific.*[215]

They reached San Francisco in early January and found news that Maling's daughter had recovered, just as the spirits said. There were a few inconsistencies with the details, but Maling blamed that on the evil spirits that had intruded during the seances. He was so convinced by end of the voyage that he practiced to become a medium himself.[216]

The Penobscot Marine Museum holds numerous logbooks and journals of Cape Horn voyages, including Searsport's Theodore P. Colcord's from aboard the *A.J. Fuller*. There are logbooks from the guano ships that rounded Cape Horn to visit Chincha Islands off Chile, including one from the *Corinne* (1853–54); an anonymous journal from aboard the bark *Alexander* of New London (1854–57); one from the ship *Wellfleet* (1862–63); and a journal by Jonathan C. Nickels from the *Moonlight* (1868–69). Another logbook with Cape Horn descriptions is from the *Rappahannock*'s March 1891 voyage under Captain Wiley R. Dickinson. There is an account titled *Sailing Along with the James Caskie 1849–50*—Newburyport captain O.O. Jones's and wife Hannah's descriptive log entries about doubling the Cape Horn.[217]

The Maine Maritime Museum has several paintings regarding Cape Horn. An oil painting from unknown artist called *Ships* Commodore *and* Donati *off Cape Horn, August 6, 1863* shows two vessels with shortened sails in a snowstorm off the cape. The *Donati* has been abandoned; there is one lifeboat alongside *Commodore*, and another struggles to make it there. Another oil painting by an unknown artist shows U.S. frigate *Congress* rounding Cape Horn in heavy seas in November 1848. A 1933 oil painting by artist Charles Robert Patterson (1875–1958) depicts the ship *Henry B. Hyde* in heavy weather off the Horn on a westward passage.[218]

Henry Hyde off Cape Horn. *Courtesy of the Maine Maritime Museum.*

Bath's museum also holds watercolors connected with the Horn. One by John Faunce Leavitt is of clipper *Live Yankee* rounding the cape.[219] There is a series of seventeen pieces of a panorama entitled *Gold Rush Voyage from Portland, ME.* Painted around 1850, one, *Ho for California*, depicts a vessel flying a flag and may represent the only full-rigged ship known to have departed Portland for California in the year following gold discovery, the 318-ton *Andrew Scott.* After its arrival, it became a storeship and never left. The ninth of the series shows a vessel flying the U.S. flag among icebergs near Cape Horn. A tenth scene depicts a ship sailing among more ice in an open ocean, while the eleventh shows two vessels in heavy seas, one with bare masts, trying to steer clear of each other and a large iceberg in the center.[220]

The Penobscot Marine Museum has an oil painting titled *Clipper Ship in Heavy Squall* by marine artist James E. Buttersworth. The painting is set in

Clipper Ship in Heavy Squall, by James E. Buttersworth, PMM catalogue No. 1979.79.23.1. *Courtesy of the Penobscot Marine Museum.*

the 1850s, with Maine-built clipper ships driving windward around Cape Horn. Buttersworth painted the vessel running with little canvas, mostly reefed topsails and a fore staysail. The crew is pictured working to take in the jib.[221]

Other ephemeral material from Cape Horn at the Maine Maritime Museum includes an 1877 navigational chart in two pieces titled *South Pacific Ocean Comprised Between the Parallels of 27 South and 60 South, and Extending from Melbourne to Cape Horn.* It is from the collection of Maine captain John Fulton Brown of Yarmouth and is filled with the navigational tracks that were made around Cape Horn in the bark *H.J. Libby* between the years 1890 and 1895. There is also a collection of papers from Captain Melvin H. Walker, consisting of fourteen letters, four envelopes and four accounts pertaining to his command of the ship *Olive S. Southard* (1874–1887). This collection includes correspondence about shipping conditions off of Cape Horn. There is also an 1849 wooden sea chest with ply rope handles, which has been associated with an 1849 Horn voyage in family history.[222]

Other Cape Horn–related items in the Penobscot Marine Museum include a sea chest that belonged to Captain Warren G. Priest, who was a deep-water sailor for forty years. An inscription states that the chest

Sea chest of Captain Warren G. Priest. *Photograph by Charles H. Lagerbom, from the Penobscot Marine Museum.*

made numerous trips around the Horn and five trips around the world. The museum also has a piano that is credited with having made the Cape Horn voyage.

Cape Horn has also been reflected in poetry. Maine Maritime Museum holds a handwritten poem by Joseph D. Williams titled "My Affectionate Memory." He wrote it to memorialize his sailor brother, Almon H. Williams, who, in 1864, was lost overboard the *Jennie Eastman* off Cape Horn. Williams wrote the poem that year and made it acrostic, in which the first letter of each line forms his brother's name. Other information about Almon Williams's death was written along the border of the poem. In its collections, the museum also has a 1975 Cape Horn Christmas card poem written by an E.R. Warren. The Thomaston Historical Society holds poems and written music about the Cape Horn ship *Alfred D. Snow*, especially its later demise on the rocks off Ireland. [223]

The Penobscot Marine Museum holds a great account entitled *Our Wedding Trip Around Cape Horn by Georgia Maria Gilkey*. On October 3, 1906, Mainer Gilkey married Phineas Banning Blanchard, and for their honeymoon, they departed from Philadelphia aboard the English-built 1866 three-mast iron ship *Bangalore* for a year-long trip around Cape Horn and back. On December

A mounted Cape Horn pigeon at the Penobscot Marine Museum. *Courtesy of the Penobscot Marine Museum.*

22, Gilkey saw Cape Horn in dead calm waters. Then they faced nothing but bad weather; one storm was so bad that she remembered the ship taking on quite a bit of water. "We seemed all that week, and many of the following, to vary between gales, head winds and dead calm." The return trip was stormy but not like it was on their way out.[224]

Another collection item is a mounted Cape Horn pigeon, often found only off the Horn in high latitudes. It dates from 1875 and was made by the second mate of the ship *Great Admiral.* The ship, named for Civil War admiral David Farragut, was captained for twelve years by Winterport's Benjamin Thompson, who may have been the original owner of the stuffed pigeon. The *Great Admiral* foundered in a storm in the Pacific in 1906.[225]

In music, Cape Horn is represented by sound, images and broader cultural links to time, identity, deity, landscape, folklore and tradition. There is Gordon Lightfoot's "Ghosts of Cape Horn" as well as the Corrie Folk Trio's "Around Cape Horn" from *The Promise of the Day* double CD. The Black Band performs an original song written by one of its members, Patrick Michael Karnahan. He wanted to give the song a rich maritime feel, like being on the deck of a rolling ship off the Horn, complete with wind and waves.[226]

For many young Maine men, the lure of escaping the farm for the sea was strong. Like a siren call, Cape Horn beckoned and challenged them. This was captured in the lyrics of "Around the Wild Cape Horn":

I was born a land-bound farm boy and in New England raised.
The rippling of the wheat fields, well they were my ocean waves.
Each rise and fall, each cry and call, of the crows across the corn
Were seagulls swooping around the bow
Of the ship I dreamed I'd sail around Cape Horn.

There, they were confronted with reality of the place, its wind, waves and weather—everything in whirling movement. How many yearned to be back on their Maine farm?

Mountain waves like avalanches, crashed upon the decks.
The screaming winds ripped ropes and spars and tried to have us wrecked.
But she rose and fell through foam and swell, her sails all ripped and torn.
Eight thousand tons, tossed like a cork
We made it 'round the wild Cape Horn.

Surviving the ordeal earned entry into an exclusive fraternity, and it also taught basic lessons of life and death and risks. Cape Horn proved a rite of passage as well as a physical passage. For Mainers and the growing United States, it represented a coming of age, ready to face one's challenges.

Well, she had us sort of hypnotized.
No time to catch our breath.
If you want to love your life, well you have to flirt with death.
Sail close to the harnessed wind and treat all risks with scorn.
A farm boy and an unyoked team
Ploughed their way around the wild Cape Horn.[227]

Even when Cape Horn was explored by film, there have been Maine connections. Producer Jim Donaldson was approached by maritime archaeologist Peter Throckmorton in the 1970s to help document them bringing the Maine-built down-easter *St. Mary* from the Falklands back to the state. Film crews departed for the islands in March 1978. What started as a simple documentary quickly expanded to a recorded history of the Cape Horn sailing ship experience. Subsequently traveling the world, Donaldson

A piano at the Penobscot Marine Museum that made the Cape Horn voyage. *Photograph by Charles H. Lagerbom.*

interviewed Cape Horn captains and crew and visited the few remaining vessels that had doubled the Horn. Directed by Keith Critchlow, the documentary was narrated by actor Jason Robards. *Ghosts of Cape Horn* aired in 1980, and television anchorman and mariner Walter Cronkite called it "true wine from man's greatest sea adventure." Gordon Lightfoot's song of the same name accompanied the film.[228] Donaldson said:

> *We began to feel, understand that we were traveling in very special company. All these people knew each other, worked with each other in a shared heritage. I think they feel closer to each other than they do to people they see every day. You…hear how men were drowned on deck driving these great ships through heavy seas, or how* [one] *fell from aloft in exhaustion in a gale and was laid out for dead in the forecastle.*[229]

8
THE END OF AN AGE

She still lies there accepting the waves of time on her beaches.
—*Thomas Wells*

The Searsport Colcords' last ship was the *State of Maine*, a down-easter launched in Newcastle in October 1878. Put in the Australian trade engaged to carry case oil or kerosene to Asia, it made the China run for the last time in 1902. The *State of Maine* had been a profitable participant in the Cape Horn trade. By 1902, however, even Captain Lincoln A. Colcord knew the end of an era was at hand. "I have felt that might be our last long voyage, and that what I struck out and worked for all my early life has become a thing of the past." In 1909, the *State of Maine* burned to its waterline, ending its days as the converted schooner barge *Scully*. Lincoln R. Colcord and his sister Joanna became instrumental in the creation of the Penobscot Marine Museum in Searsport. Born in a stormy passage off of Cape Horn in 1883, he died in Searsport in 1947.[230]

By the end of the nineteenth century, some Maine vessel owners tried to make square-riggers economically viable again, returning to passages, including Cape Horn. Bath's Arthur Sewall Company studied possibilities, especially after 1898, when the United States gained control of the Philippines, Samoa and Guam after the Spanish-American War. On an experimental voyage in 1901, the five-mast Sewall-built steel ship *Kineo* sailed from Norfolk with a load of coal for the new U.S. Navy base at Subic Bay. Not far behind was another Sewall ship, the four-mast steel bark *Edward Sewall*. Both went out by way of the Cape of Good Hope.[231]

Captain Frank W. Patten of the *Kineo* reported they did fine in the trade wind belt but struggled in long swells running down its easting. This caused sails to slat and tear in addition to breaking the boom and gaff jaws. During gales, Patten shortened the canvas to avoid having to handle the huge sails with his decks awash, which was dangerous since schooner sails were handled from the deck, not aloft. The *Kineo* worked around the Pacific with a fouled bottom, a terrible typhoon, a lack of fresh food and a crew with beriberi. It finally sailed for Philadelphia in May 1906 with three tons of sugar. Problems continued to plague the ship as it made an eastward doubling of Cape Horn, including the failure of its boiler, which meant it had no steam, heat, steam pumps or steam-hoisting engines to help haul sails. This made it the largest hand-puller schooner in the world, a severe drain on the energies of the *Kineo*'s already small and mostly ill crew. Patten reported to the owners that his experience around Cape Horn was what every other big schooner would likely go through. He convinced them that no other great schooner should attempt the route again.[232]

There is a photograph at the Penobscot Marine Museum of square-rigged ship called the *Benjamin F. Packard*. Launched on November 11, 1883, by Goss, Sawyer & Packard of Bath, it faced such extreme temperatures when rounding Cape Horn that its running gear froze in the blocks. For fifteen days, the crew was unable to effectively work the ship. Later, under Captain Zachary Allen, the *Benjamin F. Packard* was considered one of the last wooden square-riggers to double Cape Horn and survive afloat later than any other down-easter but one. It was destroyed in 1939. The 1874 Bath-built *St. Paul* was on the West Coast until 1942. At the Maine Maritime Museum, there is a wooden model of the *Benjamin F. Packard* that was built by George A. Beaumont. *Benjamin F. Packard* ended its career in New York and was scuttled in Long Island Sound in 1939. Many artifacts were salvaged off of it, including the officers' quarters, which have been exhibited at the Mystic Seaport Museum.[233]

The opening of Panama Canal in 1914 no longer put a high priority on doubling Cape Horn. Perhaps it is rather fitting the first ship to pass through the canal was a Maine-built down-easter. Also, by World War I, fully developed American transcontinental railroads and the appearance of submarines off the eastern coast both challenged Maine commercial shipping. By end of the nineteenth century, steam-powered iron vessels pushed wooden sailing vessels off world trade routes, relegating them to short runs in out-of-the-way locales. Down-easters took part in the Pacific Coast lumber trade and the Alaskan salmon fishery, and others had their masts

Maine-built steel ship *Kaiulani* was one of the last full-rigged sailing ships to round Cape Horn. *Calisphere, public domain.*

removed to serve as barges. Others were left to rot on beaches and mud flats. It is suggested that by 1915, most mariners had agreed that square-rigged sailing ships were obsolete and that their time around Cape Horn was over. By the 1920s, the focus was on iron shipbuilding, which created a ripple effect of last efforts through the Maine wooden shipbuilding yards, which ended with the Great Depression and World War II. By then, most of the ships that had been engaged in the Cape Horn trade were either sunk, sold for scrap, used as barges or lay rotting, like the *St. Mary* or the *Snow Squall* in the Falklands or the *Kaiulani* in the Philippines.[234]

The very last Maine-built square-rigger to round Cape Horn appears to have been the *Kaiulani*, when, in December 1941, it carried a load of Douglas fir from Aberdeen, Washington, to Durban, South Africa. The *Kaiulani* was a Bath iron bark built in 1899, one of the thirteen iron or steel square-riggers of the total three thousand produced in America. Owned by Arthur Sewall & Company, it was named for Victoria Kawekiu Kaiulani, the heir to Hawaii's throne. It became the *Star of Finland* in 1910 as part of the Alaska fleet until the outbreak of World War II, when it took a cargo of timber to South Africa. Captain H.G. Wigsten kept a journal of that trip from Aberdeen to Durban to Hobart, Tasmania. Sailing under Panama's flag, this was the last American crew to double Cape Horn in a commercial square-rigged sailing vessel. That December, the twenty-man crew, while off the Horn, heard news of Japan's attack on Pearl Harbor from a crewman's portable radio. On Christmas night, they crossed 50 degrees south latitude on their northward leg, the last American-owned commercial sailing ship to double Cape Horn.[235]

After its final voyage to Australia, the *Kaiulani* was used as an Allied barge in World War II's New Guinea campaign. After the war, it was used as a log barge in the Philippines until the 1960s. The National Maritime Historical Society (NMHS) was formed to preserve the *Kaiulani*. The NMHS was even appointed as a trustee of the bark by President Lyndon Johnson in 1964, after it had been presented to the United States by the Philippine government. In 1972, the Smithsonian Institution offered a $5,000 prize for a model of the *Kaiulani* for its permanent collection and display in its new Hall of American Maritime Enterprise. Recognized for its Cape Horn history, the *Kaiulani* was considered of value as "a representative steel square-rigged ocean carrier of the turn of the century and because she symbolizes the close of the age of sail for the American merchant marine and the American ship building industry." At the time, it lay at Mariveles in Subic Bay. That year, the NHMS worked to restore the *Kaiulani* in time for America's bicentennial. It would

then sail along the East Coast as a sail training ship operating out of South Street Seaport Museum.[236]

But the plans changed, even after a visit to the wreck in the 1960s by First Lady Johnson. The funding did not materialize. Eventually, only the remains of seven sections were landed at Seattle's Todd Shipyard, including the stem, stern and keel. It was called a tragedy, as no "American boy [will stand] upon her decks and revel in the fact that his forebears had conceived, designed, built and sailed this magnificent creature over all the oceans of the world under the Stars and Stripes." Only its bow went on display in 1982 at San Francisco's National Maritime Museum at the entrance to the Hyde Street Pier, near Fisherman's Wharf.[237]

EPILOGUE

A LATTER-DAY *HERO*

She ain't much fer pretty, but she sure is hell fer stout.
—visitor to the Hero *in the early 2000s*

By the 1960s, early Operation Deep Freeze expeditions had given way to more elaborate scientific involvement for America in the Antarctic. As broad-based enquiry morphed into more strategic and localized investigations, the need arose for specially designed research vessels to address these questions. When the National Science Foundation (NSF) requested a specially built, custom-designed research vessel for just such purposes to work along the Antarctic Peninsula, it turned to Maine, whose long history of wooden ship construction was still recognized into second half of the twentieth century. The result was the construction of the research vessel *Hero*, the first ship to be based in Antarctica. This modified trawler was one of the last wooden ships built in South Bristol and constructed by a team of "oldsters," old-school masters of wooden shipbuilding. The ship's caulker was eighty-six years old. The *Hero* was built for Cape Horn waters and beyond.[238]

A driving figure in the *Hero*'s story was Maine resident Jack Crowell. John Thomas "Jack" Crowell Jr. was a master mariner born in 1898 in Gloucester, Massachusetts. He survived a torpedoed ship in World War I, served on sailing ships around Cape Horn and became a polar expert, joining Donald MacMillan and his wooden schooner *Bowdoin* on trips to the Arctic in the 1920s and 1930s. He served in Greenland in World

War II, helped establish an air base at Frobisher Bay and taught airmen Arctic survival skills along the slopes of Mount Katahdin in Maine. After the war, Crowell worked on ice islands in the Arctic, surveyed sites for the DEW (Distant Early Warning) stations in northern Canada and helped establish Thule Air Base in Greenland. By the early 1960s, he was working for the NSF on polar projects, such as the research ship *El Tanin*. In January 1964, he participated in a survey search aboard icebreaker USCGS *Eastwind* to the Antarctic Peninsula.[239]

In July 1966, after the initial designs by Stanley Potter, a construction contract was awarded to the Harvey F. Gamage Shipyard in South Bristol. As the NSF representative and project supervisor for the *Hero*, Crowell rented a small house nearby and oversaw the construction phase.

Others involved included University of Maine biology professor John H. Dearborn and NSF special projects officer Bob Dale. Dearborn helped with the installation of science equipment, notably the oceanographic gear. Dale was a major background figure in the *Hero*'s daily life and relieved Crowell when he retired as the *Hero* project officer in late 1967.[240] According to Dale, Potter and Crowell were old friends from Damariscotta, where Crowell had lived and Potter owned a summer home. Even though wooden shipbuilding was on the decline, Crowell insisted on a sailing ship with wooden-hull construction. Gamage and his shipyard were well known for quality wooden vessels, and Potter and Crowell were both aware of this. A wooden ship with 160 square meters of sail was envisioned to maintain control if propulsion systems failed and reduce roll and noise during oceanographic operations. It needed to withstand yearly crossings of the Drake Passage and research in Cape Horn waters. It is suggested Crowell had romantic historical interests involved with the procurement source and design.[241]

NSF representative Ken Moulton said the sails were required early on in the planning. "From the start of the project, the concept was to build a 'quiet' ship that would not only benefit marine research operations, but also radio science projects that were planned for the future. The sails were an important part of the concept, while at the same time, benefiting fuel consumption."[242] He went on to note that there were not many shipyards in the mid-1960s interested or capable of handling a wooden sailing ship contract. "Once it was decided that a small wooden ship would best suit our needs, we were very limited as to where and who would build it. My memory is that the Gamage Yard was the only place that expressed an interest in doing the job. I believe it turned out to be a sole source contract in the end."[243]

U.S. Navy officers and NSF bigwigs gather for the launching of *Hero*, March 28, 1968. *From the Bob Dale collection, courtesy of the Antarctican Society.*

Potter noted that Crowell's demand for a wooden ship "and nothing else" carried a lot of weight, since a less-expensive steel shallow-draft, ice-strengthened hull could have been produced, but that was just not going to happen with Crowell in charge. With Crowell at the helm, building a wooden-hulled sailing ship in Maine at Harvey Gamage's shipyard seemed the perfect and, arguably, only option.[244]

Potter worked closely with Dale to gain an understanding of the conditions the *Hero* would face. They studied past Cape Horn and polar vessels, determining hull lines and structural factors. They even used early computer analysis for hull form. Dearborn recalled that Gamage was brutally blunt to visiting dignitaries, who ventured from Washington, D.C., to South Bristol during construction phase. "You can't do that," "we don't build it that way" or "we're going to do it right" were phrases Dearborn fondly recalled hearing from the old shipbuilder in his thick down-east accent. Dale, who had retired from the U.S. Navy after having participated in Operation Deep Freeze, came to like the mid-Maine coast so much during the *Hero*'s construction phase that he permanently relocated to the Brunswick area. As he periodically monitored progress of the *Hero*, Dale ventured around the coast, and that was when he decided to move there. He said his assignment was to understudy Crowell, who was soon to retire as the supervisor of the project.[245] By late 1967, Crowell had officially retired from the NSF, and Dale was the new *Hero* project officer.

Diesel-driven but equipped with sails, the wooden ship was sheathed in stout tropical greenheart from Guyana, South America. Framed with native oak timbers, the trawler's mast was made of Oregon fir. Greater thickness and closer spacing of framing distinguished it from other vessels. The eighteen-by-eighteen-inch keel was spaced only eight inches apart from its six-by-six-inch framing. The two-inch-thick oak planking was overlain with metal plating. The vessel was ketch-rigged, in addition to two 380-horsepower diesel engines on a single propeller shaft.[246] The

Hero was officially christened and launched into Damariscotta River amid much fanfare at high tide on March 28, 1968. Crowell, Dale, Potter, Moulton and Gamage were all on hand for the event. As ship began to slide, Mrs. Leland J. Haworth, the wife of the NSF director, smashed a bottle of champagne against its bow. Dale, who had just flown in from new Palmer Station and its own commissioning, was on hand to witness the event. He noted that as *Hero* "slid down the ways in the huge, ancient construction shed, bands blaring and the throng cheering, her superstructure just nicked the overhead frame of the giant doors and white clouds of 100-year-old pigeon poop drifted down from the rafters on to the applauding naval officers in their dress blues and civilian dignitaries in their finest."[247]

The *Hero* arrived November 11, 1968, at Valparaiso, after transiting the Panama Canal and picking up supplies, more equipment and scientists. It began its scientific studies at Puerto Montt, studying whales and porpoises along the coast. The cetacean study continued until it reached Punta Arenas, the last stop before the Antarctic Peninsula. The cruise in southern Chilean waters lasted from early November to early December. It was also hoped that its pelagic and benthic probes of waters around Cape Horn and peninsula would prove or disprove the existence of latent major fisheries. The *Hero* proved to be a good listening platform for Dr. Kenneth S. Norris, a senior scientist aboard. Recordings were obtained during these "silent ship" operations from both porpoises and South American sea lions.[248] Proceeding to Palmer Station, the ship departed Cape Horn waters to cross the Drake Passage on December 21. Howard wrote that the crossing lived up to its reputation. "Tried to set mizzen sail but line aloft chafed through. Tried to set storm trysail, but chafing, too. Mainsail very uncertain, so have not tried to set it. Wind about 30 or better. Rough. Could and probably will get worse."[249]

From April to May 1969, the *Hero* worked for the U.S. Bureau of Commercial Fisheries to test the feasibility of collecting near-surface krill in the mid-winter Southern Ocean. It took a month to rig and calibrate the gear. For some reason, the exercise was discontinued after a few days of trawling in the Straits of Magellan. According to one source, the gear was unrigged without further investigation of krill, fish or problems in the twine.[250] John Lohr was the radio operator aboard the *Hero* from 1974 to 1978. On the way to Cape Horn, Lohr recalled that the *Hero* did not have its full complement of new sails and had to motor most of the way.

Maine-built NSF research vessel *Hero* in Drake Passage, south of Cape Horn. *From the collection of Bob Dale, courtesy of the Antarctican Society.*

> *As we approached the roaring 40's, the weather grew more intense. It became impossible to sit upright in my chair in the radio room, so I found I could operate from the deck by wedging myself between the operating console and the bulkhead....As we passed the cape, I could see nothing but mountainous waves and heavy mist hanging on the horizon. Cape pigeons and storm petrels were the only sign of life we could see, letting us know we were near land. I was to pass this point 13 times before my 4 years working on Hero was finished.*[251]

Captain Peter Lenie's log recorded a particularly tough northern crossing of the Drake Passage in April 1973. He noted at 1000 that they faced force-7 heavy seas and swells. Two hours later, the winds increased to force 7 or 8, swells broke heavy and snow lowered visibility to zero. Spray froze on contact, and they were covered in ice. At 0330 the following morning, they lost the forestaysail in a wind gust measuring eighty knots. It took the crew three hours to secure sails. At 0600, the galley stove light fixture exploded, starting a fire, which was soon brought under control. By 1800, the seven- to ten-meter

swells, which had pounded them the entire day, prompted Lenie to write that all hands were getting tired. It was difficult to make headway, and it took them another two days to finally pass Cape Horn and head north to Isla Nuevo. By 1975, the *Hero* had made thirty-six voyages, supporting scientific research, to the Antarctic Peninsula, the South Shetland Islands and Cape Horn waters. The ship had remained in the Southern Hemisphere since its arrival in 1968, with just one visit north of the equator. In 1974, the *Hero* was sent to Long Beach, California, for an overhaul. Another major yard period happened in the 1976–77 season, but it only became apparent during the following season. During yard time, both main engines had received major overhauls.[252]

David C. Martin sailed the *Hero* in 1977, when it underwent a refit in Talcahauno, Chile. A large amount of dry rot had been found in its bow, and shipyard workers used adzes to chip away at the timbers, shaping them to replace rotted wood. Martin noticed sap spraying from the timbers as they chipped—the wood was uncured and green. This created later problems, as the wood never swelled like cured wood would have when submerged in sea water. As the *Hero* was refloated, a steady, permanent leak came in through the bow. Lenie named it *Rio Betzel* in honor of the NSF bureaucrat who had arranged the repairs. Martin wrote that they were north of Cape Horn late at night when the *Hero* hit a huge storm, which parted their mizzen. The other two able seamen, the *Hero*'s first and second mates, and Martin headed to the stern to secure the shredded sail before it wrapped up the radar. A large stainless-steel D-ring dangerously whipped back and forth in the howling wind. While fighting to secure the sail, Martin saw out of the corner of his eye something white towering over them. He yelled, gripped a stay and grabbed hold of his nearest shipmate as a huge wave broke over everyone, nearly washing them away. They eventually stowed the sail, retreating back inside the *Hero* to dry off. When they reached the actual Horn, it was found that the turbocharger after-cooler cores of both engines had been replaced during refit with freshwater cores rather than salt. As a result, both started massive leaks on this final trip north from Palmer Station to Ushuaia. As a result, Lenie had to shut down the engines. In a rather fitting coda, the *Hero* went one last time around Cape Horn under sail power.

According to Gary Bennett, who was also aboard, the engineers could not do anything underway.

> *When we couldn't make headways towards Ushuaia, just like Captain Bligh in the Bounty,* [Captain] *Lenie turned away towards Isla Estatos, where we could anchor and work on the engine. The Palmer diesel mechanic,*

The status of sunken *Hero*, November 2020. *Courtesy of the* Chinook Observer, *Long Beach, Washington.*

> *who had been unconscious for the past three days due to mal del mar, was woken and was able to assist in the repairs. He laid hands on the engine and it was healed. We were underway the next day.*[253]

The *Hero*'s later life was a sad decline. It bounced from owner to owner in the Pacific Northwest as different groups tried to utilize the vessel for a floating museum, tourist attraction or charter cruise. Nothing proved successful. The *Hero* went to public auction by the State of Oregon in 1999 and was sold for $5,000. Private ownership proved to be no better, and its final owner allowed the *Hero* to rot in Bay Center, Washington. A 2017 storm partially sank it at dock, creating a costly oil spill hazard. As of November 2020, the vessel sits in mud, slowly but surely breaking apart. It's rather an ignominious end for such a large participant in Maine maritime and Cape Horn history.[254]

NOTES

Introduction

1. Stanford, "Cape Horn Road, Part 1," 11–12; Maine Maritime Museum, "Mills Portrait"; Maine Maritime Museum, "Rock and a Wet Place."
2. Packard, *Went to Sea*, 257; Berube, personal communication with author, December 2020; Penobscot Marine Museum, "Lincoln Ross 'Link' and Captain Lincoln A. Colcord."
3. Protheroe, "Letter."

Chapter 1

4. Stanford, "Cape Horn Road, Part IX," 33; Randier, *Men and Ships*, 24–26.
5. Stanford, "Cape Horn Road, Part X," 10–11; Bell, *Seamen*, 153–55; Murphy, *Rounding the Horn*, 210; Aker, "Francis Drake," 12–13; "Note," *Sea History*, 13; "Letters," *Sea History*, 6.
6. Randier, *Men and Ships*, 48–54; Stanford, "Cape Horn Road, Part XII," 6–7.
7. Vairo, *Shipwrecks*, 32–33; Randier, *Men and Ships*, 83–88; Stanford, "Cape Horn Road, Part XV," 8.
8. Murphy, *Rounding the Horn*, 206–7, 209–10.
9. Ibid., 207; Atlas Obscura, "Monument."
10. *Allegro Blog*, "Monument."

11. Watson, *Birds*, 85–87; Todd, *Birds & Mammals*, 16; De La Pena and Rumboll, *Birds*, 5.1, 5.2; Packard, *Went to Sea*, 295–96; Randier, *Men and Ships*, 292.
12. Wells, "Odyssey," 63; Leon Gautier, quoted in Randier, *Men and Ships*, 7; Wells, "There Were None," 22–23.
13. Vairo, *Shipwrecks*, 43–44.
14. Ibid., 44–46.
15. Ibid., 49.
16. Clark, *Clipper Ship*, 161, 299; Cutler, *Greyhounds*, 161, 191–92, 200.
17. Clark, *Clipper Ship*, 190–91; Cutler, *Greyhounds*, 191–92, 249, 418, 481, 488.
18. Vairo, *Shipwrecks*, 49; Rowe, *Maritime History*, 216–17.
19. Humiston, *Blue Water*, 130–31, 132–33; Stanford, "Cape Horn Road, Part XXI," 11.
20. Wells, "Odyssey," 59; Murphy, *Rounding the Horn*, 264; Apollonio, *Last of the Cape Horners*, 163–65; Vairo, *Shipwrecks*, 44.
21. Stanford, "Cape Horn Road, Part I," 12; Crowe, "Downeasters," *Fishermen's Voice*, 1–2.
22. Packard, *Went to Sea*, 323.
23. Ibid., 323.
24. Ibid., 190–91; Maine Maritime Museum, "*Red Jacket*"; Rowe, *Maritime History*, 216–18.
25. Murphy, *Rounding the Horn*, 225–26.
26. International Maritime Library, "*Peri*"; and Murphy, *Rounding the Horn*, 227.
27. "The Ghost Ship of Cape Horn," *Daily Democrat*, April 3, 1907; *Strange Ago*, "Ghost Ship."
28. Jack Williams, "Stonie Jameson's Journal Around the Horn in 1892–1893," *Thomaston Historical Society* (1996): 8–9.

Chapter 2

29. Stanford, "Cape Horn Road, Part XVI," 11, 12.
30. "Racing Around," *Bulletin of the Business Historical Society*, 13; Fairburn, *Merchant Sail*, 1:101.
31. Cutler, *Greyhounds*, 54, 76.
32. Samuel Eliot Morison, quoted in "Racing Around," *Bulletin of the Business Historical Society*, 12; Bell, "Short-Lived Clippers"; Dean, *Snow Squall*, 7.
33. Cutler, *Greyhounds*, 41; Laing, *Seafaring America*, 88–89; Thwing, *Crooked and Narrow*, 182.

34. Whaling History, "Obed Paddack"; Headland, *Antarctic Expeditions*, 88; *Deceased Friends*, 69–72; Whaling History, "Charles F. Coffin"; National Maritime Digital Library, "*Washington*"; Whaling History, "Benjamin C. Gardner"; National Maritime Digital Library, "*Martha*"; Druett, *She Captains*, 165–67.
35. National Maritime Digital Library, "*Wiscasset*"; Lipfert, "Whalers"; Dorsett, "Whalers," 15; Rice, *Shipping Days*, 165, 167; Chase, *Wiscasset*, 417; Martin, "Voyages," 47; Martin, *Whalemen*, 26, 27; National Maritime Digital Library, "*Tyleston*"; Headland, *Antarctic Expeditions*, 164–65; Decker, *Whaling Industry*, 74; *Nantucket Whalers*, 42, 43, 45; Baker, *Maritime History*, 2:1,078.
36. Martin, "Spirit Voices," 45; Densmore, *Halo*, 151, 159, 163, 164–65, 168, 179; Martin, *Whalemen*, 34, 35.
37. Barman, "Kanakas?," 6; Barman, *Maria Mahoi*, 12.
38. Cloud, *Enoch's Voyage*, 333–34.
39. National Maritime Digital Library, "*Henry Kneeland*"; Lipfert, "Whalers"; Lawrence, *Captain's Best Mate*, 181, 188; National Maritime Digital Library, "*Lucretia*"; Mystic Seaport Museum, "Shanghaiers"; Bockstoce and Botkin, "Pacific Walruses," 185; Bockstoce, *Whales, Ice & Men*, 212, 257, 309; Baker, *Maritime History*, 2:1,097.
40. National Maritime Digital Library, "*Mary and Susan*"; Owen, "Archive"; National Maritime Digital Library, "Voyages of Owen"; Bockstoce, *Whales, Ice & Men*, 133, 141, 212, 214.
41. Samuel Eliot Morison, quoted in "Racing Around," *Bulletin of the Business Historical Society*, 10.
42. Pickering Family History, "*Flying Scud*"; Bell, "Short-Lived Clippers."
43. Hostin, "*Redemptora*."
44. Bunting, *Live Yankees*, 93–97.
45. Testimony quoted in Bunting, *Live Yankees*, 99.
46. Ibid.
47. Bunting, *Live Yankees*, 101–6.
48. Black, *Searsport*, 106; Penobscot Marine Museum, "Daniel Smith Goodell Jr."; Humiston, *Blue Water*, 97, 98, 100, 103.
49. Howe and Matthews, *Clipper Ships*, 1:52; Whipple, *Clipper Ships*, 61.
50. De Pastino, "Shipwrecks Discovered."
51. Howe and Matthews, *Clipper Ships*, 2:385–86.
52. *Republican Journal* (January 1872), quoted in "History from the Past" *Maine Coastal News* 19, no. 14 (September 2006): 5; "*Barkentine Holliswood*," Belfast Historical Society and Museum.
53. Rowe, *Maritime History*, 216, 217; Black, *Searsport*, 28–29.

Chapter 3

54. Munson, *Penobscot*, 134–35; Reid, "Gold Rush," 34.
55. *Republican Journal* (December 20, 1848); Wasson and Colcord, *Sailing Days*, 265; Maine Memory Network, "Bangor Quartette Club"; *New York Herald*, February 5, 1849; SFgeneaology, "California Bound."
56. Maine Genealogy, "Torrey"; Find A Grave, "Crabtree"; Haskins, *Argonauts*, 486; Shepard and Caldwell, *Addresses*, 6–7.
57. *Republican Journal* (March 1849); SFgeneaology, "California Fever"; WorthPoint, "Nautical Watercolor."
58. *Republican Journal* (June 1849).
59. *Republican Journal* (December 20, 1852).
60. Lagerbom, "Belfast"; Reid, "Gold Rush," 34.
61. Kinney, *Vessels*, 34, 40–41, 56.
62. Ibid., 83, 100.
63. Ibid., 107, 119; Maritime Heritage Project, "Barks, Brigs and Ships"; Rowe, *Maritime History*, 170; Bunting, *Live Yankees*, 65–66.
64. Black, *Searsport*, 77, 79, 80, 169–70.
65. Kinney, *Vessels*, 120; *Rockland Gazette*, January 6, 1854, reprinted in Overlock, *Windships*, 94; Penobscot Marine Museum, "Nathaniel Wass."
66. Biscoe, *Merchant of the Medomak*, 31, 85–86, 101–2; Cutler, *Greyhounds*, 424, 434, 488, 502; Howe and Matthews, *Clipper Ships*, 2:722–24.
67. Packard, *Went to Sea*, 220.

Chapter 4

68. Murphy, *Rounding the Horn*, 253.
69. Kinney, *Vessels*, 90; Cutler, *Greyhounds*, 157, 177, 240–45, 352, 412–13, 486, 479–80, 488, 513; Howe and Matthews, *Clipper Ships*, 1:7, 259.
70. Cutler, *Greyhounds*, 157, 230–31, 257, 333, 336, 420, 479, 484, 497; Howe and Matthews, *Clipper Ships*, 1:130–32, 182–88, 2:401–2; Snow, *Main Beam*, 59–60; Munson, *Penobscot*, 135.
71. Cutler, *Greyhounds*, 276, 420, 489, 496, 501, 507, 511, 514, 519; Howe and Matthews, *Clipper Ships*, 1:200–204; Fairburn, *Merchant Sail*, 1, 985–86.
72. Kinney, *Vessels*, 126; Cutler, *Greyhounds*, 428, 491.
73. Cutler, *Greyhounds*, 421, 488, 494, 502; Howe and Matthews, *Clipper Ships*, 1:239–40.

74. Howe and Matthews, *Clipper Ships*, 1:9–11; Cutler, *Greyhounds*, 490, 502, 511, 516, 519; Snow, *Main Beam*, 117; Fairburn, *Merchant Sail*, 2,006.
75. Cutler, *Greyhounds*, 425, 501, 511; Howe and Matthews, *Clipper Ships*, 1:43–45; Biscoe, *No Pluckier*, 49; Biscoe, *Merchant of the Medomak*, 87, 88.
76. Cutler, *Greyhounds*, 434, 507, 515; Howe and Matthews, *Clipper Ships*, 2:709–10; Fairburn, *Merchant Sail*, 2,017.
77. Rowe, *Maritime History*, 178–79; Cutler, *Greyhounds*, 332, 427, 449, 491, 501, 507, 511, 515; Howe and Matthews, *Clipper Ships*, 1:195–97; Bell, "Short-Lived Clippers"; Fairburn, *Merchant Sail*, 2,017; Wasson and Colcord, *Sailing Days*, 436.
78. Read the Plaque, "*Viking*"; Cutler, *Greyhounds*, 288, 494, 500, 510, 515.
79. Cutler, *Greyhounds*, 289, 328, 349, 433–34, 427, 509, 511; Howe and Matthews, *Clipper Ships*, 1:218–20, 2:679–81, 711–14; Fairburn, *Merchant Sail*, 2,007.
80. Munson, *Penobscot*, 136; Cutler, *Greyhounds*, 371, 432, 452, 492, 497, 520; Howe and Matthews, *Clipper Ships*, 2:610–12; Humiston, *Blue Water*, 48.
81. Cutler, *Greyhounds*, 304; Whipple, *Clipper Ships*, 99.
82. Kinney, *Vessels*, 131; Cutler, *Greyhounds*, 304, 431, 496, 501; Howe and Matthews, *Clipper Ships*, 2:509–11.
83. Overlock, *Windships*, 77–78; Cutler, *Greyhounds*, 435, 513; Howe and Matthews, *Clipper Ships*, 2:110–11.
84. Munson, *Penobscot*, 136; Cutler, *Greyhounds*, 333, 348–49, 436–37, 439, 443, 495, 505, 509–10, 512, 516, 518–20; Howe and Matthews, *Clipper Ships*, 1:167–69, 2:385–86, 656–58, 743–45; Snow, *Main Beam*, 111, 119–21; Fairburn, *Merchant Sail*, 2,007.
85. "Heroine," *New York Daily Tribune*, quoted in Maritime Heritage Project, "Joshua Patten, Mary Patten"; Humiston, *Blue Water*, 146–49.
86. Kinney, *Vessels*, 70; Cutler, *Greyhounds*, 360, 423, 488, 512, 516; Howe and Matthews, *Clipper Ships*, 1:489–90.
87. Nolte and May, "Shipwreck."
88. Crowe, "Downeasters," *Fishermen's Voice*, 1–2.
89. *Rockland Democrat and Free Press*, May 15, 1861, and September 1861, reprinted in Overlock, *Windships*, 89; Kinney, *Vessels*, 19; Snow, *Main Beam*, 93–94.
90. Bunting, *Live Yankees*, 136, 162; Garcia, "Con Radar."
91. Bunting, *Live Yankees*, 168–69.
92. Biscoe, *Merchant of the Medomak*, 57.
93. Emerson, "Round the Horn."
94. Packard, *Went to Sea*, 190.
95. Biscoe, *Merchant of the Medomak*, 93–94, 95.

96. Fred Dyer, quoted in Bunting, *Live Yankees*, 261.
97. "Letter Captain James F. Murphy to Arthur Sewall—December 15, 1895" in Snow and Lee, *Shipyard in Maine*, 101.
98. Bunting, *Live Yankees*, 294.
99. Fairburn, *Merchant Sail*, 3:1,764–765.
100. Chapman, quoted in Bunting, *Live Yankees*, 427–28.
101. Penobscot Marine Museum, "*Shenandoah*."
102. A.J. Thornley, quoted in Bunting, *Live Yankees*, 374.
103. Bunting, *Live Yankees*, 308.
104. Ibid., 365; and William Dunphy, quoted in Bunting, *Live Yankees*, 256.
105. Bunting, *Live Yankees*, 439.
106. Ibid., 439, 440, 443.
107. Ibid., 460–61.
108. Black, *Searsport*, 29.
109. Bunting, *Live Yankees*, 456.
110. Black, *Searsport*, 17; Cutler, *Greyhounds*, 233–34, 305, 471, 482, 493, 499.
111. Buttersworth, "*Warner*."
112. Bunting, *Live Yankees*, 149; Black, *Searsport*, 182–83.
113. Cutler, *Greyhounds*, 485, 492; Howe and Matthews, *Clipper Ships*, 1:96–101; Kinney, *Vessels*, 58.
114. Cutler, *Greyhounds*, 249, 423, 463, 487, 511, 515; Howe and Matthews, *Clipper Ships*, 2:504–6; Snow, *Main Beam*, 60; Fairburn, *Merchant Sail*, 2,015.
115. Kinney, *Vessels*, 120.
116. Snow, *Shipyard in Maine*, 50; Bunting, *Live Yankees*, 475; Packard, *Went to Sea*, 227.
117. Penobscot Marine Museum, "*Polly*."
118. Penobscot Marine Museum, "Journal of P.B.F. Bassatt of Brig *Francisco*."
119. Biscoe, *Merchant of the Medomak*, 30, 31.
120. Penobscot Marine Museum, "Jeremiah Grant Park"; Black, *Searsport*, 158.
121. *Republican Journal* (January 1872), quoted in "History from the Past," *Maine Coastal News* 19, no. 14 (September 2006): 5; Carter, "Carter Papers"; Gebert, *Carters of Woolwich*, 17–20.
122. Penobscot Marine Museum, "Clifton Curtis"; Black, *Searsport*, 73–74; Humiston, *Blue Water*, 82–83.
123. History Link, "Captain William Talbot."
124. Singer, "Whaling Ship"; History Link, "*Fresno*"; Bunting, *Live Yankees*, 166.
125. Mitchell, "Journal."
126. Ibid.
127. Ibid.

128. Ibid.
129. Steven Hutchings, personal communication with the author, December 2020; Banel, "First State Representative"; *Republican Journal* (September 29, 1994): A17.
130. SCRET, "*A.J. Fuller*"; Stanford, "Cape Horn Road, Part II," 12; Maine Maritime Museum, "*A.J. Fuller*"; Penobscot Maritime Museum, "Captain Theodore."
131. Stanford, "Cape Horn Road, Part XII," 6–7.
132. Riesenberg, *Cape Horn*, 197.
133. Ibid., 198.
134. Ibid., 199.

Chapter 5

135. Ibid., 2.
136. *Portland Christian Mirror*, March 27, 1851; Dean, *Snow Squall*, 18.
137. Snow, *Main Beam*, 107–8, 114–15, 124.
138. Kinney, *Vessels*, 29.
139. Nowell, "Nowell Legacy."
140. Ibid.
141. Packard, *Went to Sea*, 242; Thomaston Historical Society, "Genealogy."
142. Vairo, *Shipwrecks*, 38; *Portland Daily Press*, September 21, 1891, 1; Tromp, *Pactolus Bank*, 4, 9, 13–14, 22.
143. From an account by descendant Flora M. Putnam (March 1985), Thomaston Historical Society; York, "*Alfred D. Snow*."
144. Biscoe, *No Pluckier*, 27.
145. Packard, *Went to Sea*, 193.
146. Black, *Searsport*, 29, 39, 55, 175–76.
147. Bunting, *Live Yankees*, 376, 433–34.
148. Ibid., 82, 84, 159.
149. Ibid., 167–68; Penobscot Marine Museum, "*El Capitan*."
150. Bunting, *Live Yankees*, 283–84; Penobscot Marine Museum, "Log of Ship *Rappahannock*"; Penobscot Maine Museum, "Wreck of the Ship *Rappahannock*," catalogue no 1952.34.
151. Black, *Searsport*, 32, 40, 43, 66; Packard, *Went to Sea*, 224; Bunting, *Live Yankees*, 315.
152. Omar Humphrey, quoted in Bunting, *Live Yankees*, 192.
153. Ibid.; Matthews, *Merchant Ships*, 253–56.

154. Bunting, *Live Yankees*, 192.
155. Ibid., 383, 386, 416, 423.
156. Black, *Searsport*, 91; Megan Pinette, personal communication with the author, November 23, 2020; Applebee, *Sailing Vessels*, 8–14; Bunting, *Live Yankees*, 454.
157. Black, *Searsport*, 48.
158. Find A Grave, "Jesse Thayer Carver"; Carver, "Mezlar Carver"; Low and Throckmorton, "Voyage of the *St. Mary* Pt II," 15, 16.
159. Low and Throckmorton, "Voyage of the *St. Mary* Pt II," 13; *Bath Daily Times*, May 23, 1890.
160. "Minot Papers—Personal Letters, Series IV" from Weigle, *Inventory*, 3; Beegan, "Sole Surviving Piece," 23; Low and Throckmorton, "Voyage of the *St. Mary* Pt II," 13; Low and Throckmorton, "Voyage of the *St. Mary* Pt I," 8; Scrimshaw Gallery, "John Stobart"; Sefton, "*St. Mary*."
161. Low and Throckmorton, "Voyage of the *St. Mary* Pt I," 9.
162. Weigle, *Inventory*, 12; Low and Throckmorton, "Voyage of the *St. Mary* Pt II," 13; Sefton, "*St. Mary*."
163. Low and Throckmorton, "Voyage of the *St. Mary* Pt II," 14; Weigle, *Inventory*, 12.
164. "Copy of Letter from Jesse Thayer Carver to Evelina W. Nichols Carver 1890," Manuscript Collection MS-90, Charles V. Minott Shipyard, Bath: Maine Maritime Museum, box no. 157, folder 17; Low and Throckmorton, "Voyage of the *St. Mary* Pt II," 14.
165. "Copy of Letter from Jesse Thayer Carver to Evelina W. Nichols Carver 1890," Manuscript Collection MS-90, Charles V. Minott Shipyard, Bath: Maine Maritime Museum, box no. 157, folder 17.
166. Low and Throckmorton, "Voyage of the *St. Mary* Pt II," 15.
167. Packer, "Report," 16–17; Low and Throckmorton, "Voyage of the *St. Mary* Pt II," 15; Sefton, "*St. Mary*."
168. Manuscript Collection MS-90, Charles V. Minott Shipyard, Bath: Maine Maritime Museum, box no. 157, folders 20, 21, 22, 23, 24; Low and Throckmorton, "Voyage of the *St. Mary* Pt II," 15; Sefton, "*St. Mary*."
169. Black, *Searsport*, 48; Low and Throckmorton, "Voyage of the *St. Mary* Pt II," 15–16; Weigle, *Inventory*, 15.
170. *Falkland Islands Magazine*, September 1890, 3; Berryman, communication with the author, December 28, 2018; Low and Throckmorton, "Voyage of the *St. Mary* Pt II," 15; Black, *Searsport*, 48; Find A Grave, "Jesse Thayer Carver."

171. Berryman, communication with the author, December 28, 2018; Low and Throckmorton, "Voyage of the *St. Mary* Pt I," 7.
172. Low and Throckmorton, "Voyage of the *St. Mary* Pt II," 15; Sefton, "*St. Mary*"; Weigle, *Inventory*, 15.
173. Weigle, *Inventory*, 12, 101–2, 141.
174. Berryman, communication with author, December 28, 2018; Scrimshaw Gallery, "John Stobart."
175. Throckmorton, "American Heritage," 40; Sefton, "*St. Mary*"; Berryman, communication with the author, December 28, 2018.
176. Berryman, *Kraut*, 160.
177. Sefton, "*St. Mary*"; Low and Throckmorton, "Voyage of the *St. Mary* Pt I," 7; Berryman, *Kraut*, 160.
178. Sefton, "*St. Mary*"; Berryman, *Kraut*, 163.
179. Berryman, *Kraut*, 162–63.
180. Berryman, communication with the author, December 28, 2018; Throckmorton, "Beast," 28.
181. Berryman, communication with the author, December 28, 2018.
182. Throckmorton, "Beast," 28; Sefton, "*St. Mary*"; Beegan, "Sole Surviving Piece," 23; Berryman, *Kraut*, 167.
183. Berryman, communication with the author, December 28, 2018.
184. Ibid.
185. Berryman, *Kraut*, 167–68.
186. Cleaves, "Maine Sailing Ship," 10; Berryman, communication with the author, December 28, 2018; Sefton, "*St. Mary*"; Beegan, "Sole Surviving Piece," 23.
187. Cleaves, "Maine Sailing Ship," 10; "Letter, Paul Rivard to Eric Berryman," in Berryman, *Kraut*, 169–70; "Concerns," *Sea History*, 32.
188. Cleaves, "Maine Sailing Ship," 10.
189. Berryman, *Kraut*, 165.
190. Beegan, "Sole Surviving Piece," 23; "*St. Mary* Salvage," *Sun Journal*; Berryman, communication with the author, December 28, 2018; Berryman, *Kraut*, 162.
191. Berryman, *Kraut*, 159–60.
192. Dean, *Snow Squall*, 10, 14, 62–63; Bell, "Short-Lived Clippers."
193. Dean, *Snow Squall*, 40, 50, 64, 67, 70, 72.
194. *Alta California*, August 3, 1853; Dean, *Snow Squall*, 96–97.
195. Dean, *Snow Squall*, 130, 133, 134, 136; Maritime History Virtual Archives, "*Snow Squall*."

196. Rowe, *Maritime History*, 174–75; Cutler, *Greyhounds*, 292, 356–57, 489; Howe and Matthews, *Clipper Ships*, 2:582–85; Bell, "Sailing Ships"; *New York Times*, September 16, 1863; Stanley, *Logs*, ix, 46–47; Dean, *Snow Squall*, 172–76, 178, 179, 180, 181, 184.
197. Albert Dibblee Papers, "Statement," C-G 180, 41; Dean, *Snow Squall*, 186.
198. Dean, *Snow Squall*, 189, 191, 192, 193, 194, 197; Howe and Matthews, *Clipper Ships*, 2:585; Smith, *Condemned at Stanley*, 22–23; Enyon, *Beneath Falkland*, 176; Throckmorton, "American Heritage," 37.
199. Dean, *Snow Squall*, ix, 213; Throckmorton, "American Heritage," 39.
200. Dean, *Snow Squall*, 214, 216, 221, 222–23, 244, 265, 268, 269; Maritime History Virtual Archives, "*Snow Squall*"; Bell, "Short-Lived Clippers."
201. Penobscot Marine Museum, "Charles Melvin Nichols"; Black, *Searsport*, 137; Riesenberg, *Cape Horn*, 193–97; Wasson and Colcord, *Sailing Days*, 301.

Chapter 6

202. Vairo, *Shipwrecks*, 44–46, 112–13.
203. Rowe, *Maritime History*, 170–72.
204. Charles Waite, "Journal—January 30, 1850," quoted in Vairo, *Shipwrecks*, 167–68.
205. Ibid., 168.
206. Jones, *Chronology*, 1–3, 4.
207. Ibid., 4–6.
208. Ibid., 6–7, 9–12.
209. Ibid., 12–15.
210. Ibid., 15–16.
211. Ibid., 16–17.
212. Ibid., 17, 22–23; Davidson, "Sea."

Chapter 7

213. Kipling, "Long Trial"; Dana, *Two Years*, 26; London, "Westing."
214. *Old News from Southern Maine*, "Captain Maling."
215. Ibid.
216. Ibid.

217. "Journal of Theodore P. Colcord of Searsport," Ms no. 332, Ms no. 333, Ms no. 334, PMM; Logbooks and Sea Journals at the Penobscot Marine Museum, Searsport, Maine 04974, compiled by Wayne M. O'Leary (July 1972); Penobscot Marine Museum, "Sailing Along."
218. Maine Maritime Museum, "Ships *Commodore* and *Donati*"; Maine Maritime Museum, "U.S. Frigate *Congress*"; Patterson, "*Henry B. Hyde*."
219. John Faunce Leavitt, "Clipper Ship *Live Yankee* Rounding Cape Horn," Maine Maritime Museum catalogue no. 86.039.5, www.maritimeme.pastperfectonline.com.
220. Maine Maritime Museum, "Gold Rush Voyage."
221. Buttersworth, "Heavy Squall."
222. Maine Maritime Museum, "South Pacific Ocean"; Maine Maritime Museum, "Walker Papers"; Maine Maritime Museum, "Sea Chest."
223. Williams, "Memory"; Warren, "Christmas Card."
224. Gilkey, "Our Wedding Trip."
225. Penobscot Marine Museum, "Stuffed Bird."
226. Critchlow, *Ghosts*; Corrie Folk Trio, "Around Cape Horn," posted by mandolinda6 on April 27, 2010, www.youtube.com; Black Irish Band, "Rounding Cape Horn," posted by Patrick Karnahan on January 5, 2011, www.youtube.com.
227. AZLyrics, "Around the Wild Cape Horn."
228. Critchlow, *Ghosts*; Cronkite, "Ghosts," 11.
229. "'Ghosts of Cape Horn,'" *Sea History*, 33.

Chapter 8

230. Biscoe, *No Pluckier*, 77; Bell, "Sailing Ships"; Munson, *Penobscot*, 291.
231. Snow and Lee, *Shipyard in Maine*, 271.
232. Bunting, *Live Yankees*, 458–60; Snow and Lee, *Shipyard in Maine*, 271–72; Fairburn, *Merchant Sail*, 1,808–810.
233. Rowe, *Maritime History*, 216–18; Penobscot Marine Museum, "*Benjamin F. Packard*"; Maine Maritime Museum, "*Benjamin F. Packard* Model," catalogue no. 2004.064.1, www.maritimeme.pastperfectonline.com.
234. Crowe, "Downeasters," *Fishermen's Voice*, 1–2; Bell, "Sailing Ships"; Murphy, *Rounding the Horn*, 265.
235. Stanford, "Cape Horn Road, Part XIX," 10; Stanford, "Cape Horn Road, Part XXI," 12; Edward LeBlanc, "Kaiulani Logbooks Discovered," National Park Service, www.nps.gov; Thomas, "*Kaiulani*," 37.

236. Stanford, "Cape Horn Road, Part XIX," 10; Stanford, "Cape Horn Road, Part XXI," 12; "Smithsonian," *Sea History*, 6, 31; Stanford, "Ships of San Francisco," 10–11.
237. Stanford, "Update," 3; Stanford, "President's Report," 1; Bliese, "Aloha," 3, 33; Carr, "Trust," 16; "Ship Notes," *Sea History*, 42; Hutchinson, "Letters," 4; Stanford, "Lost *Kaiulani*," 6.

Chapter 9

238. Eberhart, "Antarctica Under Sail," 628; Dale, personal communication with the author, March 29, 2011.
239. "John Thomas Crowell Jr., Obituary," *Arctic*, 292; Palmer Station, "Old Palmer."
240. Manning, "*Hero*," 1C; Bob Dale, personal communication with the author, August 15, 2014; Moulton, personal communication with the author, August 15, 2014.
241. Spindler, personal communication with the author, August 14, 2014.
242. Moulton, personal communication with the author, August 15, 2014.
243. Ibid.
244. Dale, personal communication with the author, August 15, 2014; Morrison, personal communication with the author, August 27, 2014.
245. Dearborn, audio interview: 2179b, February 17, 2009; Dale, personal communication with the author, March 29, 2011.
246. "*Hero*," *Antarctic Journal of the United States*, 58–59; Eberhart, "Antarctica Under Sail," 629; Dale, personal communication with the author, August 15, 2014.
247. Dale, personal communication with the author, March 29, 2011.
248. Norris, "First *Hero* Cruise," 163–64; Eberhart, "Antarctica Under Sail," 629; Manning, "*Hero*," 1C; Manning, "Scientists," 2C.
249. Howard, "*Alfred D. Snow*," 6C.
250. Manning, "Scientists," 3C.
251. Ibid.
252. Mulcahy, "*Hero*," 65–66, 69.
253. Gary Bennett and Bill Spindler, personal communication with the author, August 28, 2014; *Summary of Cruise* 78-1C, (March 13, 1978–July 9, 1978).
254. Matt Winters, personal communication with the author, November 19, 2020; Spindler, personal communication with the author December 5, 2020; Lagerbom, "Antarctic Hero," 36–60.

BIBLIOGRAPHY

Aker, Raymond. "Francis Drake at Cape Horn." *Sea History*, no. 80 (Winter 1996–97): 12–13.

Allegro Blog. "Cape Horn Monument." www.allegro.mncarpenters.net.

Alta California. August 3, 1853.

Apollonio, Spencer. *The Last of the Cape Horners: Firsthand Accounts from the Final Days of the Commercial Tall Ships*. Washington, D.C.: Brassey's, 2000.

Applebee, Robert. *Sailing Vessels Built in Belfast*. Belfast, ME: Belfast Historical Society and Museum.

Atlas Obscura. "Cape Horn Monument." www.atlasobscura.com.

AZLyrics. "Around the Wild Cape Horn." www.azlyrics.com.

Baker, William A. *A Maritime History of Bath, Maine, and the Kennebec River Region*. 2 vols. Bath, ME: Marine Research Society of Bath, 1973.

Banel, Feliks. "How King County's First State Representative Disappeared in Mysterious Shipwreck." October 9, 2019. www.mynorthwest.com.

Barkentine Holliswood. Belfast, ME: Belfast Historical Society and Museum.

Barman, Jean. *Maria Mahoi of the Islands*. Ottawa, CA: New Star Books, 2004.

———. "Whatever Happened to the Kanakas? They're Alive and Well in British Columbia." *Beaver: Exploring Canadian History* 77, no. 6 (December 1997/January 1998): 6–7.

Bassatt, P.B.F. "Journal of P.B.F. Bassatt of Brig *Francisco*." Penobscot Marine Museum.

Bath Daily Times. May 23, 1890.

Beegan, D. "Sole Surviving Piece of Historic Sailing Ship St. Mary Returning." *Lewiston Daily Sun*, June 23, 1978.

Bell, Douglas. *Elizabethan Seamen.* Philadelphia: J.B. Lippincott Company, 1936.

Bell, Tom. "Short-Lived Clippers Were Built for Speed, Profit." *Portland Press Herald*, June 10, 2007. www.mainetoday.com.

———. "When Sailing Ships Ruled, Maine Was Global Player." *Portland Press Herald*, June 3, 2007. www.mainetoday.com.

Bennett, Gary. Personal communication with the author, August 28, 2014.

Berryman, E. *The Kraut: On Being German After 1940.* Virginia Beach, VA: CreateSpace Independent Publishing, 2015.

———. Personal communication with the author, August 2018.

Berube, John F. Personal communication with the author, December 2020.

Biscoe, Mark W. *Merchant of the Medomak: Stories from Waldoboro Maine's Golden Years 1860–1910.* Waldoboro, ME: Waldoboro Historical Society, 2004.

———. *No Pluckier Set of Men Anywhere: The Story of Ships and Men in Damariscotta and Newcastle.* Newcastle, ME: Lincoln County Publishing Co., 2001.

Black, Frederick Frasier. *Searsport Sea Captains.* Searsport: Penobscot Marine Museum, 1960.

Black Irish Band. "Rounding Cape Horn." Posted by Patrick Karnahan on January 5, 2011. www.youtube.com.

Bliese, Joachim. "Aloha *Kaiulani.*" *Sea History*, no. 5 (Autumn 1976): 3, 33.

Bockstoce, John R. *Whales, Ice & Men: The History of Whaling in the Western Arctic.* Seattle: University of Washington Press, 1995.

Bockstoce, John R., and Daniel B. Botkin. "The Harvest of Pacific Walruses by the Pelagic Whaling Industry, 1848 to 1914." *Arctic and Alpine Research* 14, no. 3 (1982): 185–86.

Bunting, W.H. *Live Yankees: The Sewalls and Their Ships.* Bath: Maine Maritime Museum, 2009.

Buttersworth, James Edward. "Clipper Ship in Heavy Squall by James E. Buttersworth." Penobscot Marine Museum, catalogue no. 1979.79.23.1.

———. "Clipper Ship *Warner* Rounding Cape Horn." Maine Maritime Museum, catalogue no. 93.85. www.maritimeme.pastperfectonline.com.

Carr, Frank G.G. "Towards a World Ship Trust." *Sea History*, no. 7 (Spring 1977): 16.

Carter, Edward L. "Carter Papers." Maine Maritime Museum, catalogue no. MS-004. www.maritimeme.pastperfectonline.com.

Carver, Jesse Thayer. "Copy of Letter from Jesse Thayer Carver to Evelina W. Nichols Carver 1890." Manuscript Collection MS-90, Charles V. Minott Shipyard, Bath: Maine Maritime Museum, box no. 157, folder 17.

———. "Jesse Thayer Carver." www.ancestors.familysearch.org.

Carver, Mezlar. "Mezlar Carver." www.ancestors.familysearch.org.

Catalogue of Nantucket Whalers and Their Voyages from 1815 to 1870. Nantucket, MA: Hussey & Robinson, 1876.

Chase, Fannie. *Wiscasset in Pownalborough: A History of the Shire Town and the Salient Historical Features of the Territory Between the Sheepscot and Kennebec Rivers.* Wiscasset, ME: Anthoensen Press, 1967.

Clark, Arthur Hamilton. *The Clipper Ship Era.* New York: G.P. Putnams' Sons, 1910.

Cleaves, H. "Maine Sailing Ship Limped to Falklands." *Bangor Daily News*, April 6, 1982.

Cloud, Enoch Carter. *Enoch's Voyage: Life on a Whale Ship 1851–1854.* Providence, RI: Moyer Bell, 1994.

Colcord, Lincoln. "Lincoln Ross 'Link' and Captain Lincoln A. Colcord." Catalogue no. LB2003.61.44. Penobscot Marine Museum, Sweetser Collection.

Colcord, Theodore P. "Journal of Theodore P. Colcord of Searsport." Ms no. 332, Ms no. 333, Ms no. 334, PMM.

"Concerns of the Ship Trust Committee." *Sea History*, no. 14 (Summer 1979): 32.

Critchlow, Keith F., dir. *Ghosts of Cape Horn*. Produced by Keith F. Critchlow and James R. Donaldson III. Posted by MaineiacNorth, 2020. www.youtube.com.

Cronkite, Walter. "'Ghosts of Cape Horn' Observed." *Sea History*, no. 16 (Winter 1980): 11.

Crowell, John Thomas. "John Thomas Crowell Jr., Obituary." *Arctic* 43, no. 3 (September 1990): 292.

Crowe, Mike. "Downeasters; Belaying Pin Soup at the Roaring Forties." *Fishermen's Voice* 10, no. 3 (March 2005): 1–2. www.fishermensvoice.com.

Cutler, Carl C. *Greyhounds of the Sea: The Story of the American Clipper Ship.* Annapolis, MD: United States Naval Institute, 1967.

Dale, Bob. Personal communication with the author, March 29, 2011, and August 15, 2014.

Dana, Richard Henry. *Two Years Before the Mast.* New York: HarperCollins, 1840.

Davidson, Carla. "Down to the Sea." *American Heritage* 56, no. 3 (June/July 2005): 16–17. www.americanheritage.com.

Dean, Nicholas. Snow Squall*: The Last American Clipper Ship.* Bath: Maine Maritime Museum, 2001.

Dearborn, John H. Audio interview: 2179b. February 17, 2009.

Decker, R.O. *Whaling Industry of New London*. York, UK: G. Schumway, 1986.

De La Pena, Martin R., and Maurice Rumboll. *Birds of Southern South America and Antarctica.* Princeton, NJ: Princeton University Press, 1998.

Densmore, David C. *The Halo: An Autobiography*. Boston: Voice of Angels Publishing House, 1876.

De Pastino, Blake. "Shipwrecks Discovered in Nautical 'Graveyard' at San Francisco's Golden Gate." *Western Digs*, December 31, 2015. www.westerndigs.org.

Dibblee, Albert. "Statement of General Average and Special Charges, Case of the Ship *Snow Squall*." Albert Dibblee Papers, Bancroft Library, University of California at Berkeley, C-G 180, 41.

Dorsett, E. Lee. "The Maine Whalers." *Down East* 11, no. 4 (April 1956): 15.

Druett, Joan. *She Captains: Heroines and Hellions of the Sea*. New York: Simon & Schuster, 2001.

Eberhart, Jonathan. "Antarctica Under Sail: Sails and a Wooden Hull Open Ways to the Bottom of the World." *Science News*, December 21, 1968, 628.

Emerson, John Brown. "Round the Horn by Captain John." Typed manuscript, Penobscot Marine Museum.

Enyon, David. *Beneath Falkland Island Waters: Marine Life, Shipwrecks, Diving.* Stanley, Falkland Islands: South Atlantic Publications, 2009.

Fairburn, William Armstrong. *Merchant Sail.* 6 vols. Center Lovell, ME: Fairburn Marine Educational Foundation Inc., 1945–55.

Falkland Islands Magazine, September 1890, 3.

Find A Grave. "George T. Crabtree" www.findagrave.com.

———. "Jesse Thayer Carver." www.findagrave.com.

Garcia, Richard. "Con Radar e Inmersiones Arqueólogos Rastrean la Flota Guanera Perdida de Pabellón de Pica." *El Mercurio*, November 2019.

Gebert, Avis Carter. *The Carters of Woolwich, Maine: A History of a Family and a Town and the Sea*. Bloomington, IN: Traford Publishing, 2008.

"The Ghost Ship of Cape Horn." *Daily Democrat*, April 3, 1907.

"'Ghosts of Cape Horn': The Genesis of a New Film on the American Heritage in Sail." *Sea History*, no. 14 (Summer 1979): 33.

Gilkey, Georgia Maria. *Our Wedding Trip Around Cape Horn*, 1906–7. Penobscot Marine Museum.

Haskins, C.W. *The Argonauts of California by a Pioneer.* Sacramento: California Genealogy & History Archives, 1890.

Headland, R.K. *Chronological List of Antarctic Expeditions and Related Historical Events.* Cambridge, UK: Cambridge University Press, 1989.

"*Hero*: A New Antarctic Research Ship." *Antarctic Journal of the United States* 3, no. 3 (May–June 1968): 53–60.

"History from the Past." *Maine Coastal News* 19, no. 14 (September 2006): 5.

History Link. "Captain William Talbot Establishes a Steam Sawmill at Port Gamble in July 1853." www.historylink.org.

———. "Vessel *Fresno* Burns in Meydenbauer Bay on April 4, 1923." www.historylink.org.

Hostin, Geraldo. "The Clipper Ship *Redemptora*, 1851–1898: A Study in Archaeology, History and Heritage Management." Master's thesis, professional archaeology, Harvard University, May 2018.

Howard, Judson. "R/V HERO, Antarctic Expedition." *National Fisherman* 51, no. 1 (January 1971): 4C–7C, 16C, 22C.

Howe, Octavius T., and Frederick C. Matthews. *American Clipper Ships 1833–1858*. 2 vols. New York: Dover, 1986.

Humiston, Fred. *Blue Water Men—And Women.* Portland, ME: Guy Gannett Publishing Co., 1965.

Hutchings, Steven. Personal communication with the author, December 2020.

Hutchinson, Alan. "Letters." *Sea History*, no. 47 (Summer 1988): 4.

International Maritime Library. "*Peri*." www.internationalmaritimelibrary.org.

Jones, Priscilla. *Chronology of the Ship P.R. Hazeltine 1875–1882*. Searsport: Penobscot Marine Museum, 1982.

Kinney, Joyce E. *The Vessels of Way Down East.* Bangor, ME: Joyce E. Kinney, 1989.

Kipling, Rudyard. "The Long Trial." www.poetryfoundation.org.

Lagerbom, Charles H. "An Antarctic Hero: The History and Fate of the NSF Research Vessel *Hero*." *New England Journal of History* 71, nos. 1–2 (Fall/Spring 2015): 36–60.

———. "Belfast Shipbuilding." *Village Soup*, November 19, 2020.

Laing, Alexander. *Seafaring America*. New York: American Heritage History, 1974.

Lawrence, Mary Chipman. *The Captain's Best Mate: The Journal of Mary Chipman Lawrence on the Whaler ADDISON, 1856–1860*. Edited by Stanton Garner. Hanover, NH: University Press of New England, 1966.

Leavitt, John Faunce. "Clipper Ship *Live Yankee* Rounding Cape Horn." Maine Maritime Museum, catalogue no. 86.039.5, www.maritimeme.pastperfectonline.com.

LeBlanc, Edward. "Kaiulani Logbooks Discovered." National Park Service. www.nps.gov.

"Letters." *Sea History*, no. 126 (Spring 2009): 6.

Lipfert, Nathan. "Maine Whalers." Maine Maritime Museum.

Logbooks and Sea Journals at the Penobscot Marine Museum, Searsport, Maine 04974. Compiled by Wayne M. O'Leary, July 1972.

London, Jack. "Make Westing." www.americanliterature.com.

Low, S.H., and P. Throckmorton. "The First and Last Voyage of the *St. Mary*, Pt. I." *Sea History*, no. 9 (1977): 8–11.

———. "The First and Last Voyage of the *St. Mary*, Pt. II." *Sea History*, no. 10 (1978): 13–16.

Maine Genealogy. "William L. Torrey." Belfast Deaths, 1881–1885. www.archives.mainegenealogy.net.

Maine Maritime Museum. "*Benjamin F. Packard* Model." Catalogue no. 2004.064.1. www.maritimeme.pastperfectonline.com.

———. "Between a Rock and a Wet Place: Death and the Mariner." Notes from the Orlop Maine Maritime Museum. www.mainemaritimemuseum.org.

———. "Captain Melville H. Walker Papers, MS-343." Catalogue no. 2019.025.01. www.maritimeme.pastperfectonline.com.

———. "Capt. Harvey Mills Portrait." Catalogue no. 93.065.1. www.maritimeme.pastperfectonline.com.

———. "Gold Rush Voyage from Portland, ME." Catalogue no. 94.023.02, 94.023.12, 94.023.13, 94.023.14. www.maritimeme.pastperfectonline.com.

———. "*Red Jacket* Ironstone Plate." Catalogue no. 96.044. www.maritimeme.pastperfectonline.com.

———. "Sailing Card for *A.J. Fuller*." Catalogue no. 2005.070.057. www.maritimeme.pastperfectonline.com.

———. "Sea Chest." Catalogue no. 81.067.1. www.maritimeme.pastperfectonline.com.

———. "Ships *Commodore* and *Donati* off Cape Horn, August 6, 1863." Catalogue no. 65.1212. www.maritimeme.pastperfectonline.com.

———. "South Pacific Ocean Comprised Between the Parallels of 27 South and 60 South, and Extending from Melbourne to Cape Horn." Catalogue no. 2018.039.08.09a-b. www.maritimeme.pastperfectonline.com.

———. "U.S. Frigate *Congress* Capt. E.A.F. Lavalette Off Cape Horn, November 20, 1848." Catalogue no. 94.071.14. www.maritimeme.pastperfectonline.com.

Maine Memory Network. "Bangor Quartette Club, Old Hampden Town House, 1849." www.mainememory.net.

Manning, S.F. "*Hero* Tests Herself at Both Ends of World." *National Fisherman* 51, no. 1 (January 1971): 1C.

———. "Scientists Reap Harvest in *Hero*'s First Year." *National Fisherman* 51, no. 1 (January 1971): 2C.

Maritime Heritage Project. "Barks, Brigs and Ships." www.maritimeheritage.org.

———. "Joshua Patten, Mary Patten." www.maritimeheritage.org.

Maritime History Virtual Archives. "*Snow Squall*." www.bruzelius.info.

Martin, Kenneth R. "Spirit Voices and a Bath Whaler." *Down East* 20, no. 4 (November 1973): 45–46.

———. "Voyages of Maine Whaleships." *Down East* 18, no. 8 (May 1972): 46–47.

———. *Whalemen and Whaleships of Maine.* Brunswick, ME: Harpswell Press, 1975.

Matthews, Frederick C. *American Merchant Ships 1850–1900.* Salem, MA: Marine Research Society, 1930.

Memorials of Deceased Friends: Of New England Yearly Meeting. Providence, RI: Knowles & Vose, 1841.

Minot, Charles V. "Charles V. Minott Shipyard Records, 1835–1974." www.dev.mmmuseum.webfactional.com.

———. Manuscript Collection MS-90: Charles V. Minott Shipyard Records, Inclusive Dates: 1835–1974, Bulk Dates: 1854–1917. Bath: Maine Maritime Museum Library.

Mitchell, Edwin. "Journal of Edwin Mitchell of Belfast, ME." MS no. 9. Penobscot Marine Museum. www.penobscotmarinemuseum.org.

Morrison, Jay. Personal communication with author, August 27, 2014.

Moulton, Ken. Personal communication with author, August 15, 2014.

Mulcahy, Michael. "*Hero* Is 7 Years Old." *Antarctic Journal of the United States* 10, no. 3 (May/June 1975): 65–69.

Munson, Gorham. *Penobscot: Down East Paradise.* Camden, ME: Down East Enterprise, 1959.

Murphy, Dallas. *Rounding the Horn: Being the Story of Williwaws and Windjammers, Drake, Darwin, Murdered Missionaries and Naked Natives.* New York: Basic Books, 2004.

Mystic Seaport Museum. "San Francisco Shanghaiers: 1886–1890." www.library.mysticseaport.org.

National Maritime Digital Library. "*Henry Kneeland*." www.nmdl.org.

———. "*Lucretia*." www.nmdl.org.

———. "*Martha*." www.nmdl.org.

———. "*Mary and Susan*." www.nmdl.org.

———. "*Tyleston*." www.nmdl.org.

———. "Voyages of Owen, Leander C." www.nmdl.org.

———. "*Washington*." www.nmdl.org.

———. "*Wiscassett*." www.nmdl.org.

New York Daily Tribune. "A Heroine of the Sea." February 18, 1857.

New York Herald. August 5, 1857.

New York Times. September 16, 1863.

Nolte, Carl, and Meredith May. "Shipwreck Makes a Romantic Return: Remains of Clipper Ship Appear Again on Ocean Beach Every 20 Years or So." May 9, 2007. www.sfgate.com.

Norris, Kenneth S. "First *Hero* Cruise in the Southern Hemisphere." *Antarctic Journal of the United States* 4, no. 4 (July–August 1969): 163–64.

"Note on Cape Horn." *Sea History*, no. 73 (Spring 1995): 13.

Nowell, George W. "Nowell Legacy at Kennebunkport." *Old News from Southern Maine*, February 4, 2010. www.someoldnews.com.

Old News from Southern Maine. "Captain Maling Conjures the Dead." March 2, 2009.

Overlock, Leland. *Windships of Warren, Maine: Writings and Records Pertaining to the History of Shipbuilding and Related Matters, 1770 to 1867*. Brewer, ME: Leland Overlock, 1988.

Owen, Leander. "Archive of Captain Leander Owen, Legendary Whaling Master, First Steam Whaler in the Arctic." www.tenpound.com.

Packard, Aubigne Lemond. *A Town That Went to Sea*. Portland, ME: Falmouth Publishing House, 1950.

Packer, Dorothy. "Report from the Falklands." *Sea History*, no. 78 (Summer 1996): 16–17.

Palmer Station. "Old Palmer." www.palmerstation.com.

Patterson, Charles Robert. "Ship *Henry B. Hyde* Rounding Cape Horn Western Passage." Maine Maritime Museum, catalogue no. 91.108. www.maritimeme.pastperfectonline.com.

Penobscot Marine Museum. "*Benjamin F. Packard*." Catalogue no. LB2005.24.9746. Boutilier Collection.

———. "Captain Theodore Persons Colcord." www.penobscotmarinemuseum.org.

———. "Charles Melvin Nichols (1851–1937)." Catalogue no. LB2008.3.201. Ship Captains Collection.

———. "Clifton Curtis (1858–1928)." Catalogue no. LB2008.3.88. Sweetser Collection.

———. "Daniel Smith Goodell Jr. (1853–1912)." Negative Film Catalogue no. LB2008.3.144.

———. "Full Model of Ship *El Capitan*." Catalogue no. 1964.23.

———. "Jeremiah Grant Park (1849–1916)." Catalogue no. LB2008.3.246. Ship Captains Collection.
———. "Log of Ship *Corinne*." MS no. 11.
———. "Log of Ship *Rappahannock* of Bath, Me." MS no. 5.
———. "Nathaniel Wass." Catalogue no. LB2007.1.103854. Eastern Collection.
———. "Sailing Along with the *James Caskie* 1849–50."
———. "Schooner *Polly*." Catalogue no. LB2000.52.463. Coombs Collection.
———. "*Shenandoah*." Catalogue no. LB2005.24.21444. Boutilier Collection.
———. "Stuffed Bird: Cape Horn Pigeon." Catalogue no. 68.
———. "Wreck of the Ship *Rappahannock*." Catalogue no. 1952.34.
Pickering Family History. "Clipper Ship *Flying Scud*." www.pickeringhistory.com.
Pinette, Megan. Personal communication with the author, November 23, 2020.
Portland Christian Mirror. March 27, 1851.
Portland Daily Press. September 21, 1891, 1.
Protheroe, Lorena Reed. "Letter, Lorena Reed Protheroe to Lincoln Colcord, July 19, 1937." Penobscot Marine Museum.
"Racing Around Cape Horn with the California Clippers." *Bulletin of the Business Historical Society* 4, no. 3 (May 1930): 10–13.
Randier, Jean. *Men and Ships Around Cape Horn 1616–1939*. New York: David McKay Company Inc., 1966.
Read the Plaque. "American Clipper Ship *Viking*." www.readtheplaque.com.
Reid, Shelley. "The Ships of the San Francisco Gold Rush." *Sea History*, no. 90 (Autumn 1999): 34–35.
Republican Journal. December 20, 1852.
———. December 20, 1848.
———. January 1872.
———. June 1849.
———. March 1849.
———. September 29, 1994, A17.
Rice, Edmund. Diary. August 23, 1858–June 23, 1859.
Rice, George Wharton. *The Shipping Days of Old Boothbay from the Revolution to the World War, with Mention of Adjacent Towns*. Boothbay Harbor, ME: Southworth-Anthoensen Press, 1938.
Riesenberg, Felix. *Cape Horn*. London: Robert Hale, 1950.
Rockland Democrat and Free Press. May 15, 1861.
———. September 1861.

Rockland Gazette. January 6, 1854.

Rowe, William Hutchinson. *The Maritime History of Maine: Three Centuries of Shipbuilding and Seafaring*. Gardiner, ME: Harpswell Press, 1989.

SCRET. "A.J. Fuller" www.scret.org.

Scrimshaw Gallery. "John Stobart—*The St. Mary Approaching Cape Horn*." www.scrimshawgallery.com.

Sefton, J. "*St. Mary* (Shipwreck) 1890." www.shipstamps.co.uk.

SFgeneaology. "California Bound." www.sfgenealogy.org.

———. "The California Fever." www.sfgenealogy.org.

Shepard, George, and S.L. Caldwell. *Addresses of Reverend Professor George Shepard and Reverend S.L. Caldwell to the California Pilgrims from Bangor, Maine*. Bangor, ME: Smith & Sayward, printers, 1849.

"Ship Notes, Seaport and Museum News." *Sea History*, no. 25 (Autumn 1982): 42.

Singer, Natalie. "Whaling Ship May Be Bridge's Mystery Vessel." *Seattle Times*, November 4, 2003.

Smith, John. *Condemned at Stanley: Notes and Sketches on the Hulks and Wrecks at Port Stanley Falkland Islands*. Chippenham, UK: Picton Publishing Ltd., 1986.

"Smithsonian Offers $5,000 Prize for Kailuani Model Contest." *Sea History*, no.1 (April 1972): 6, 31.

Snow, Bertram G. *The Main Beam: An Informal History of Documented Vessels Built at Rockland, Maine, from 1795 to 2005*. Rockland, ME: Rockland Historical Society, 2005.

Snow, Ralph Linwood, and Douglas K. Lee. *A Shipyard in Maine: Percy & Small and the Great Schooners*. Bath: Maine Maritime Museum, 1999.

Spindler, Bill. Personal communication with the author, August 14, 2014 and December 5, 2020.

"*St. Mary* Salvage Operation Topic of Talk." *Sun Journal*, April 10, 2010.

Stanford, Peter. "The Cape Horn Road." *Sea History*, no. 70 (Summer 1994): 11–14.

———. "The Cape Horn Road, Part II." *Sea History*, no. 71 (Autumn 1994): 10–12.

———. "The Cape Horn Road, Part IX: Spain Charges Ahead—Around the World!" *Sea History*, no. 79 (Autumn 1996): 8–11, 33.

———. "The Cape Horn Road, Part X: Francis Drake Sails for Freedom." *Sea History*, no. 80 (Winter 1996–97), 8–11.

———. "The Cape Horn Road, Part XII: The River that Led Around the World." *Sea History*, no. 82 (Autumn 1997): 6–9.

———. "The Cape Horn Road, Part XV: Britain Keeps the Sea." *Sea History*, no. 85 (Summer 1998): 8–13.

———. "The Cape Horn Road, Part XVI: Columbia, the Gem of the Ocean!" *Sea History*, no. 86 (Autumn 1998): 8–13.

———. "The Cape Horn Road, Part XIX: Steamships Take Over the North Atlantic, Driving the Sailing Ship into Increasingly Remote Trades." *Sea History*, no. 89 (Summer 1999): 8–12.

———. "The Cape Horn Road, Part XXI: Here…All Men Mattered." *Sea History*, no. 91 (Winter 1999–2000), 9–13.

———. "How We Lost *Kaiulani*—and What We've Been Doing About It!" *Sea History*, no. 71 (Summer 1994): 6.

———. "President's Report." *Sea History*, no. 4 (July 1976), 1.

———. "The Ships of San Francisco: Ships Built the City and Their Heritage Challenges the City Today." *Sea History*, no. 38 (Winter 1985–86): 10–11.

———. "Update." *Sea History*, no. 3 (July 1975): 3.

Stanley, W., ed. *The Logs of the CSS* Alabama *and the CSS* Tuscaloosa, *Kept by Lieutenant John Low, CSN.* Tuscaloosa: University of Alabama Confederate Publishing Co., 1972.

Strange Ago. "The Ghost Ship of Cape Horn." August 2, 2017. www.strangeago.com.

Summary of Cruise 78-1C. March 13, 1978–July 9, 1978.

Thomaston Historical Society. "Genealogy of Watts Ship Captains from Thomaston, Warren and St. George, Maine."

Thomas, William. "Christmas Aboard the Bark *Kaiulani* 1941." *Sea History*, no. 5 (Autumn 1976): 35–37.

Throckmorton, Peter. "The American Heritage in the Falklands." *Sea History*, no. 4 (July 1976): 36–41.

———. "The Beast on the Beach" *Sea History*, no. 11 (Summer 1978): 28.

Thwing, Annie Haven. *The Crooked and Narrow Streets of the Town of Boston 1630–1822.* Boston: Marshall Jones Company, 1920.

Todd, Frank S. *Birds & Mammals of the Antarctic, Subantarctic & Falkland Islands.* Lake Worth, FL: Ibis Publishing Co., 2004.

Tromp, Hylke. "The Story of the Pactolus Bank: A Lost Island Near Cape Horn." May 2008. www.archive.org.

Vairo, Carlos Pedro. *Shipwrecks in Cape Horn: Isla de Los Estados, Magallanes, Mitre Peninsula, Malvinas and South Georgias.* Ushuaia, AR: Zagier & Urruty Publications, 2001.

Warren, E.R. "Cape Horn Christmas Card Poem." Maine Maritime Museum Catalogue no. 94.087.185 www.maritimeme.pastperfectonline.com.

Wasson, George S., and Lincoln Colcord. *Sailing Days on the Penobscot: The River and Bay as They Were in the Old Days with a Record of Vessels Built There Compiled by Lincoln Colcord.* Salem, MA: Marine Research Society, 1932.

Watson, George E. *Birds of the Antarctic and Sub-Antarctic.* Washington, D.C.: American Geophysical Union, 1975.

Weigle, Anastasia S. *Inventory for Manuscript Collection MS-90: Charles V. Minott Shipyard Records, Inclusive Dates: 1835–1974, Bulk Dates: 1854–1917.* Bath: Maine Maritime Museum Library, 2013.

Wells, Thomas. "And Then There Were None." *Sea History*, no. 29 (Fall 1983): 22–23.

———. "A Cape Horn Odyssey." *Sea History*, no. 18 (Fall 1980): 57–63.

Whaling History. "Master ID: AM1119—Charles F. Coffin." www.whalinghistory.org.

———. "Master ID: AM2089—Benjamin C. Gardner." www.whalinghistory.org.

———. "Master ID: AM3701—Obed Paddack." www.whalinghistory.org.

Whipple, A.B.C. *The Clipper Ships.* Alexandria, VA: Time-Life Books, 1984.

Williams, Jack. "Stonie Jameson's Journal Around the Horn in 1892–1893." *Thomaston Historical Society* (1996): 8–9.

Williams, Joseph D. "My Affectionate Memory." Maine Maritime Museum Catalogue no. 2018.031.05 www.maritimeme.pastperfectonline.com.

Winters, Matt. Personal communication with the author, November 19, 2020.

WorthPoint. "Signed Nautical Watercolor Bark 'Suliote' Sailing Ship." www.worthpoint.com.

York, William Howard. "*Alfred D. Snow* Reefed Down for Heavy Weather." Maine Maritime Museum Catalogue no. 2001.059.1. www.maritimeme.pastperfectonline.com.

ABOUT THE AUTHOR

Charles H. Lagerbom received his bachelor's degree in history from Kansas State University and a master's degree in history and archaeology from the University of Maine with work on a Revolutionary War truckhouse that was excavated from the Penobscot River. An avid scuba diver, Charles organized underwater surveys of ship remains in Maine lakes as well as the 1779 Penobscot Expedition. He worked in Antarctica with glacial geology research teams from the University of Maine Quaternary Institute, now the Climate Change Institute. A published author, avid polar and colonial Maine and maritime book collector, Charles is a frequent guest lecturer presenting on cruise ships, sailing vessels and ashore about history, life, politics and science of Antarctica, Cape Horn and South Atlantic, as well as colonial Maine and New England maritime history and archaeology. He is the author of *The Fifth Man: The Life of H.R. Bowers* (Caedmon Publishing, 1999) and *Whaling in Maine* (Arcadia Publishing, 2020). Charles is a past president of the Antarctican Society, where he currently serves as an archivist/historian. He publishes a weekly column in the *Camden Herald* titled "Half Seas Over: Interesting Research Related to Maritime Maine." Charles teaches AP U.S. History at Belfast Area High School and makes his home on the coast of Maine. He can be reached through LinkedIn or at clagerbom@rsu71.org.

The author off Cape Horn on a "quiet" weather day. *Photograph by Marvin Kenney, from the collection of Charles H. Lagerbom.*